THE BATHROOM BOOK OF HISTORY FACTS

1091+ STRANGE, FUNNY & FORGOTTEN TRUTHS THEY NEVER TAUGHT YOU IN SCHOOL

LUCAS RUSSO

Copyright © 2025 by Lucas Russo

All rights reserved.

No part of this publication may be copied, reproduced, stored in a retrieval system, or transmitted in any form or by any means—electronic, mechanical, photocopying, recording, or otherwise—without the prior written permission of the author, except in the case of brief quotations used for review, research, or educational purposes as permitted by law.

This is a work of original content. All information, facts, trivia, and supplementary material are based on the author's independent research or are intended for entertainment and educational use only. Any resemblance to actual persons, living or deceased, or to real events is purely coincidental unless explicitly stated.

Introduction 6
1: Bizarre Inventions Throughout History 7
    Bathroom Trivia — Fresh Flush Edition 13
    Answer: 13
2: Presidential Insights 14
    Flush-Worthy Firsts: Presidential Edition 25
3. Unbelievable Fiascos 26
    Fiasco Fallout – A Blunder Blitz! 44
    Answers: 45
4. Epic Failures In History 46
    Toilet Time Trivia: Flop or Fact? 57
    Answer 58
5. Lost Civilizations 59
    Flush: True or Poo? 73
    Answer Key: 74
6. Historical hoaxes and pranks 75
    Fool Me Once 96
    Answer: 98
7. Women who changed history 99
    Guess Who? – Women Who Changed History Edition 112
    Answer 113
8. History Of Unusual Sports 114
    Flush & Field – Sport or Satire? 120
    Flush-Worthy Answer Key: 121
9. Cultural Taboos And Their Origin 122
    "Taboo or Not Taboo?" 129
    Answers: 129
10. Revolutionary ideas that shocked the world 130
    Brainstorm Blitz: Ideas That Shook the World 137
    Ideas: 138

Answer Key: 138
11. Architecture that defied logic 139
   "Would You Build It?" Quiz 146
   Time to Unveil the Blueprints! (Answers) 147
12. Historical Events That Were Almost Forgotten 148
   Forgotten But Fantastic: 153
   Answer Key: 154
13. The Oddest Items Used as Currency 155
   Toilet Timeline Trivia: 160
   ANSWER: 160
14. Unexpected Alliances in History 161
   Toilet Time Top 3s 166
15. Weirdest Jobs People Have Done in History 168
   Bathroom Trivia — True or False? 171
   Answers: 171
   Bathroom Trivia— True or False? 171
   Answers: 171
16. Strange Historical Coincidences 172
   Flush-Worthy Firsts" 184
17. Unusual Punishments Throughout the Ages 185
   Punishment or Performance? 188
   Answers: 188
18. Strange Origin of Everyday Phrases 189
   "Say What?" – Phrase Origins Trivia Challenge 195
   Answers: 195
19. Absurd Laws That Once Existed 196
   Law or LOL? 201
   Answers: 202
20. Historical Scandals That Made Headlines 203

Bathroom Trivia: Scandal Edition 206
    Answers: 207
21. Unexpected Inventions That Shaped the World 208
    Guess the Idiot 213
    Answers: 214
Outro 215

Introduction

Welcome to the Throne Room — and no, we're not talking about Buckingham Palace. You've officially taken your seat on the most sacred porcelain pedestal, and we couldn't be more honored to join you. This book is your ultimate bathroom buddy, here to entertain while you... take care of business.

Inside these pages, you'll find the strangest, funniest, and downright dumbest moments in history. Wars started over pastries. Kings who banned beards. Emperors who appointed horses to government positions. It's all real. And it's all completely ridiculous. If you've ever thought, "History is boring," prepare to eat those words... preferably not while on the toilet.

There's no right way to read this book. Just flip to any page and dive in. Each fact is short, weird, and 100% true — the perfect companion for long sits, quick breaks, or those mysterious disappearances where your family starts asking, "Are you okay in there?"

We hope you laugh. We hope you learn. And most of all, we hope you never look at history (or your bathroom breaks) the same way again. Let's wipe away the boring and flush in the fun — one weird fact at a time.

1: Bizarre Inventions Throughout History

1925 – The Isolator Helmet
Fact: In 1925, Hugo Gernsback came up with "The Isolator"—a giant, awkward helmet designed to help writers focus by blocking out all sound… and most of their oxygen. Because apparently, nothing sparks creativity like being trapped in a soundproof bubble and slowly running out of air.

1911 – Concrete Furniture
Fact: And back in 1911, Thomas Edison thought your home needed a serious upgrade—with concrete furniture. We're talking rock-solid pianos, chairs, even cabinets. Because clearly, when you imagine cozy living, you picture a living room made of stone.

1912 – Coat Parachute
Fact: Franz Reichelt designed a coat parachute in 1912 and tested it by jumping off the Eiffel Tower. Spoiler alert: gravity won that day.

1973 – Motorized Ice Cream Cone
Fact: In 1973, Arthur Garth invented the Motorized Ice Cream Cone—a gadget that rotated the cone for you so your tongue didn't have to put in the

effort. Because apparently, licking ice cream was just too exhausting for some people.

1984 – Hay Fever Glasses
Fact: In 1984, Kenji Kawakami introduced Hay Fever Glasses—giant goggles with tissues hanging off them for those sneezes that hit at the worst times. Because nothing says "fashionable" like a pair of nose tissues swinging from your face.

1888 – Electric Belt For Men
Fact: In 1888, Dr. Sanden started selling the Electric Belt for Men—a wearable zap machine that claimed to fix everything from bad kidneys to bedroom troubles. Let's just say the results were... less than electrifying.

1912 – The Revigator
Fact: In 1912, R.W. Thomas came up with the "Revigator" — a clay water cooler lined with radium that was supposed to make your drinking water healthier by making it slightly radioactive. Yep, people were basically sipping radiation in the name of wellness.

1922 – Infant Cage
Fact: In 1922, Emma Read came up with the "Infant Cage" — a wire box that parents could hang outside their apartment windows so babies could get some "fresh air." The catch? These cages hung several stories high, right above solid concrete—because what better way to get fresh air than by hovering over a sidewalk?

1935 – Piano Bed
Fact: In 1935, Thomas Pap thought, "Why choose between sleep and music?" So, he came up with the Piano Bed—yep, an actual bed with a built-in piano. Ideal for anyone who felt the urge to play a tune in the middle of the night instead of, you know, just sleeping.

1884 – Copper Mesh Underwear
Fact: In 1884, Louis Pasteur came up with copper mesh underwear that he believed could prevent rheumatism by letting your body "breathe electricity." Yep—because apparently, electric undies were the next big health trend.

1921 – The Criminal Catcher
Fact: In 1921, Helene Adelaide Shelby came up with The Criminal Catcher, essentially a remote-controlled lasso gun for police officers too lazy to chase suspects.

1882 – Le Petit Protector (Pocket Watch Gun)
Fact: In 1882, French gunsmith Jacques Turbiaux created the "Le Petit Protector" — a tiny pistol disguised as a pocket watch. Perfect for when someone asks you the time, and you're in the mood to seriously confuse them.

1921 – Flame-Throwing Trumpets
Fact: Flame-throwing trumpets were created by Richard Paget, in 1921, to protect against gas attacks, orchestras were turned into possible weapons of war.

1931 – The Radio Hat
Fact: In 1931, Victor Hoeflich came up with the Radio Hat—a pith helmet with a built-in radio, making the idea of "wearing your music" cool long before headphones.

1936 – All-Terrain Shoe
Fact: In 1936, M.W. Hulbert invented the All-Terrain Shoe, which had small tank treads on each foot, so you could roll instead of walk.

1932 – The Cyclomer
Fact: In 1932, Julien Bender invented the Cyclomer, a bike with flotation devices meant to ride across water. Turns out, it mostly just left cyclists wet.

1911 – Duo-Plane
Fact: The "Duo-Plane," invented by Glen Curtiss in 1911, was a vehicle with detachable wings that could turn from a car into a plane. Unfortunately, it wasn't great at either—kind of like a jack of all trades, master of none.

1873 – Mustache Guard
Fact: The Mustache Guard, invented by Virgil Gates in 1873, was made to

keep facial hair free from food stains. It attached to cups, so gentlemen could drink without messing up their whiskers.

1870 – Pneumatic Tube Transit
Fact: The Pneumatic Tube Personnel Transportation System was designed by Alfred Beach in 1870. It proposed shooting people through tubes like bank deposits.

1973 – Flying Pinto
Fact: In 1973, Henry Smolinski tried to make a flying car by attaching Cessna wings to a Ford Pinto. Sadly, it crashed during testing.

1879 – Skull Excavator
Fact: In 1879, Pierre Anceaux invented the Skull Excavator, a device meant for making precise holes in skulls. It was marketed as a handy at-home medical tool—back before we had any real regulations to stop ideas like this.

1932 – Dynasphere
Fact: The "Dynasphere," invented by Dr. J.A. Purves in 1932, was a giant electric wheel where the driver sat inside the wheel rather than on top of it.

1882 – Alarm Clock Bed
Fact: The Alarm Clock Bed, created by Leonard Bailey in 1882, literally dumped sleepers onto the floor when it was time to wake up.

1929 – Extensible Bathing Gown
Fact: The Extensible Bathing Gown, created by Charles Richter in 1929, had fabric that could be pulled down from the bathing suit to the ground. This let Victorian women walk to the beach fully covered, then pull the fabric back up when they were ready to swim.

1929 – Wooden Bathing Suit
Fact: The Wooden Bathing Suit, made by the Spruce Manufacturing Company in 1929, was built from thin wooden slats held together with piano wire—because clearly, swimming in something that floats like a plank sounded safer than it actually was.

1953 – Combination Gun-Fan

Fact: The Combination Gun-Fan, dreamed up by James Williams in 1953, was exactly what it sounds like—a revolver with fan blades stuck on the barrel. Fire a shot, and the fan spins, supposedly keeping you cool while you aim. Because nothing says multitasking like staying breezy and armed.

1911 – Electrified Tablecloth

Fact: Back in 1911, Samuel Steward thought he had the perfect solution to flies ruining dinner — an electrified tablecloth that zapped any bug that landed on it. The only problem? It sometimes zapped the dinner guests too. Not exactly the kind of table shock you want with your soup.

1912 – Face-Slapping Machine

Fact: In 1912, Dr. Edmund Hooker introduced the Face-Slapping Machine — a device meant to boost circulation by, well, slapping you repeatedly. Because apparently, nothing says "radiant skin" like getting smacked by a machine.

2011 – Solar-Powered Bikini

Fact: Almost a century later, in 2011, Andrew Schneider came up with the Solar-Powered Bikini — outfitted with tiny solar panels that let you charge your phone while catching some sun. Because who wouldn't want to turn their swimsuit into a gadget?

2001 – Transparent Concrete

Fact: In 2001, Hungarian architect Áron Losonczi created Transparent Concrete — a special kind of concrete with tiny optical fibers inside that let light pass through, making solid walls glow naturally.

2005 – Invisible Bike Helmet

Fact: In 2005, Anna Haupt and Terese Alstin came up with the Hövding Invisible Bike Helmet — a wearable collar that stays hidden until you crash, then instantly inflates like an airbag to protect your head.

1994 – Baby Mop

Fact: In 1994, Mike Koffler introduced the Baby Mop — a funny little outfit covered in microfiber that let crawling babies double as floor cleaners. Because why not multitask while they explore?

2012 – Ostrich Pillow
Fact: In 2012, the Kawamura-Ganjavian studio came up with the Ostrich Pillow — a super soft, wrap-around head pillow with holes for your hands. It lets you nap anywhere, even if you end up looking like a sleepy space creature.

1931 – One-Wheeled Motorcycle
Fact: In 1931, Italian inventor M. Goventosa introduced the One-Wheeled Motorcycle. Imagine riding inside a giant wheel — that's exactly what it was! A wild concept that took "riding in style" to a whole new level.

1982 – Anti-Eating Face Mask
Fact: In 1982, Lucy Wills invented the Anti-Eating Face Mask, a device that made it impossible to eat anything. Think of it as the original "willpower in a box" — perfect for anyone who needed a little extra help sticking to their diet.

2013 – Hairy Stockings
Fact: The Anti-Pervert Hairy Stockings were created by a Chinese company in 2013, featuring realistic leg hair to avoid unwanted male attention.

1975 – Pet Rock
Fact: In 1975, Gary Dahl "invented" the Pet Rock — yep, just a rock in a carrying case with a training manual. Somehow, it sold over a million units for $4 each. Who knew a rock could be such a hit?

2008 – Keyboard Pants
Fact: In 2008, Erik De Nijs introduced the Keyboard Pants — yes, pants with a keyboard on the thighs and a mouse in the crotch area. Apparently, typing at a desk just wasn't edgy enough!

1881 – Rotary Jail
Fact: In 1881, William Brown came up with the Rotary Jail — a prison with cells arranged in a circle that rotated to line up with one door. The idea? Make sure prisoners couldn't escape in groups.

1922 – Concrete Hiking Boots

Fact: In 1922, Alexander Layman invented concrete hiking boots — weighing in at a whooping 12 pounds each and completely rigid. Because, apparently, regular blisters just weren't challenging enough.

🚽 Bathroom Trivia — Fresh Flush Edition

1. What food item was once used as currency by the ancient Aztecs?

☐ A) Tortillas ☐ C) Corn husks

☐ B) Chocolate beans ☐ D) Jalapeños

2. What did Napoleon accidentally do before a royal rabbit hunt?

☐ A) Ate all the carrots

☐ B) Fell asleep in his boots

☐ C) Released too many rabbits — and got swarmed

☐ D) Declared war on lettuce

3. Which U.S. president filed an official UFO report?

☐ A) Ronald Reagan ☐ C) Jimmy Carter

☐ B) George W. Bush ☐ D) Barack Obama

4. What bizarre "pet" did President John Quincy Adams keep in the White House?

☐ A) A talking parrot ☐ C) A raccoon in a waistcoat

☐ B) An alligator ☐ D) A goat named "Mr. President"

5. What musical instrument once used live animals (seriously)?

☐ A) Bark-o-Organ ☐ C) Moo-Synthesizer

☐ B) The Cat Piano ☐ D) Oink-a-phone

Answer:

1 – B, 2 – C, 3 – C, 4 – B, 5 – B

2: Presidential Insights

1912 – Shot Mid-Speech
Fact: Theodore Roosevelt was shot in the chest before a speech—but still spoke for 90 minutes with the bullet lodged in him. He began: "It takes more than that to kill a Bull Moose."

1995 – Pizza in Underwear
Fact: Russian President Boris Yeltsin was found outside the White House in his underwear at 3 AM, trying to get a cab for pizza during a visit to Washington.

1960s – The Oval Office Throne
Fact: President Lyndon B. Johnson often held meetings while sitting on the toilet, door open, claiming it saved time. Multitasking at its most presidential.

1913 – Taft vs. Bathtub
Fact: President Taft once got stuck in the White House bathtub and needed four men to rescue him. He later ordered an oversized tub to prevent future embarrassment.

2014 – Presidential Scooter Stealth
Fact: French President François Hollande snuck out on a scooter to visit his actress girlfriend. A helmet was his only disguise—not very stealthy.

1845 – Foul-Mouthed Funeral
Fact: At President Andrew Jackson's funeral, his pet parrot had to be removed for loudly swearing in front of mourners.

2002 – Renaming the Calendar
Fact: Turkmenistan's President Niyazov renamed January after himself and April after his mother. He also made news anchors swear their teeth would fall out if they lied.

1992 – Bushusuru Incident
Fact: President George H.W. Bush vomited on Japan's Prime Minister during dinner, creating the term "Bushusuru"—Japanese slang for public puking.

1977 – A Crown for a King
Fact: Central African President Bokassa spent a third of his country's budget on a coronation, complete with a 32-pound crown and eight-horse carriage.

1989 – Rock Music Warfare
Fact: U.S. troops blasted Van Halen outside Manuel Noriega's hideout until the former Panamanian leader surrendered. No one escapes the power of rock.

2000s   Tent Diplomacy
Fact: Libyan leader Muammar Gaddafi traveled with a Bedouin tent and a squad of female bodyguards, pitching it on hotel lawns during diplomatic visits.

1899 – Died on Active Service
Fact: French President Félix Faure died in office—literally—while receiving oral sex from his mistress. At his funeral, someone quipped, "He died as he lived: on active service."

1920s – Dear Jerry
Fact: President Warren G. Harding nicknamed his penis "Jerry" and wrote steamy letters to his mistress featuring lines like "Jerry came and will not go."

1800s – Skinny Dipping Diplomacy
Fact: President John Quincy Adams regularly skinny-dipped in the Potomac River. A reporter once sat on his clothes until he agreed to an interview.

1970s – A Title Too Far
Fact: Ugandan dictator Idi Amin gave himself the title: "Lord of All the Beasts of the Earth and Fishes of the Sea..." It went on—and on.

2009 – The Obama Excuse
Fact: When Angela Merkel scolded Silvio Berlusconi for keeping world leaders waiting, he brushed it off with, "I was calling Mr. Obama."

1970s – Magic vs. Machinery
Fact: Equatorial Guinea's dictator banned lubricants at sawmills, believing his magical powers could stop friction. The sawmill promptly burned down.

1831 – Lincoln the Wrestler
Fact: Young Abraham Lincoln won 299 of 300 wrestling matches. After one win, he told the crowd, "I'm the big buck of this lick. If any of you want to try it, come on!"

1920s – Panic Buttons and Pranks
Fact: President Calvin Coolidge enjoyed pressing White House emergency bells, then hiding to watch the staff panic.

1970s – Doing a Gerald Ford
Fact: President Gerald Ford's clumsiness was so legendary that reporters coined the phrase "doing a Gerald Ford" every time he stumbled.

2007 – Presidential Talent Show
Fact: Venezuela's Hugo Chávez hosted an 8-hour episode of his talk show

Aló Presidente, where he sang, danced, and announced policies live—without breaks.

1969 – Madman Theory
Fact: President Richard Nixon ordered bombers to fly near Soviet airspace to appear unstable, hoping to intimidate enemies by playing the "madman."

2007 – Banana Cure Thursdays
Fact: Gambia's Yahya Jammeh claimed he could cure AIDS using herbs and bananas—on Thursdays only—leading to a government-backed treatment program.

1976 – Rise of the Statue
Fact: Togo's President Eyadéma installed a statue of himself that rose from the ground to synthesizer music whenever guests arrived.

1801 – Borrowed Coat Blunder
Fact: President James Madison once showed up to a formal event wearing Thomas Jefferson's coat by accident. It was so oversized he looked like a child.

2014 – The Million-Dollar Beetle
Fact: "World's poorest president" José Mujica of Uruguay drove an old VW Beetle. When offered $1 million for it, he refused: "Are you crazy?"

1960s – Short-Leg Diplomacy
Fact: French President Charles de Gaulle had chairs with shortened legs made for guests so he'd appear taller in meetings.

2016 – Duterte's Power Nap
Fact: Philippine President Rodrigo Duterte once left world leaders waiting at a summit—for hours—because he needed a nap.

1920s – Poker and Porcelain
Fact: President Warren G. Harding lost White House china in a poker game—he bet government heirlooms that weren't his to wager.

1969 – UFO Files
Fact: Governor Jimmy Carter filed an official UFO sighting report and promised he'd never mock anyone for seeing strange lights in the sky.

1972 – Dress Code Ban
Fact: Mobutu Sese Seko of Zaire banned Western suits and names in favor of "authentic" African fashion. His leopard-skin hat became a national symbol.

1841 – Long Speech, Short Presidency
Fact: President William Henry Harrison delivered the longest inaugural address in freezing rain—then died of pneumonia 32 days later.

2014 – Werewolf Insurance
Fact: Argentine President Cristina Fernández de Kirchner adopted a Jewish boy as her godson to prevent him from turning into a werewolf—based on local legend.

1990s – The UFO Runway
Fact: Argentina's President Carlos Menem built a private landing strip at home—because he believed aliens would soon visit him.

1947 – Secret Bowling Shame
Fact: President Harry Truman secretly bowled alone in the White House basement—embarrassed by his terrible technique.

2003 – Lula's Loud Nap
Fact: Brazil's President Lula da Silva snored loudly through a G8 press conference—caught live on mic while his peers were speaking.

2015 – The Great Mugabe Trip
Fact: Zimbabwe's Robert Mugabe fell down a staircase at his 91st birthday celebration. His staff forced journalists to delete the photos.

2013 – Pistachio Diplomacy
Fact: Israel's Prime Minister Netanyahu spent $2,700 on pistachio ice cream in a single year, prompting national budget scrutiny.

2002 – Pretzel Panic
Fact: President George W. Bush fainted after choking on a pretzel while watching football. He awoke with a bruised cheek and dazed staff.

1996 – Napkin of Secrecy
Fact: French President François Mitterrand's final meal involved eating an illegal bird under a napkin—to hide the act from God.

2009 – Anthem on the Grass
Fact: After collapsing from heat exhaustion while jogging, French President Nicolas Sarkozy was found lying on the grass—singing the national anthem.

1970 – Cecilia Banned
Fact: Malawi's President Hastings Banda banned the Simon & Garfunkel song "Cecilia" because his girlfriend shared the name and he disliked the lyrics.

2011 – Pen-Gate
Fact: Czech President Václav Klaus was caught on video pocketing a ceremonial pen during a press conference—creating the international "Pen-Gate" scandal.

2015 – Locked Out
Fact: President Barack Obama once got locked out of the White House and resorted to throwing pebbles at a window to get someone's attention.

1975 – Boxing Instead of War
Fact: Uganda's President Idi Amin proposed solving a territorial dispute with Tanzania by challenging their president to a boxing match.

2006 – Cold Shower Control
Fact: South African President Jacob Zuma claimed cold showers helped him control his sexual urges—he had six wives at the time.

1998 – Tea Time Terror
Fact: During a 1998 visit, Irish President Mary McAleese accidentally poured tea in Prince Philip's lap. His startled response: "Good heavens, woman!"

2013 – Marital Distance
Fact: Afghan President Hamid Karzai admitted in 2013 that he hadn't spoken directly to his wife in over 15 years—communicating only through staff.

2015 – Steak in Style
Fact: Russian President Vladimir Putin released a workout video in a $3,200 outfit, then sat down to enjoy a steak with his Prime Minister.

WWII Era – Secret Dog Aboard
Fact: FDR smuggled his dog, Fala, aboard military ships to international conferences—despite regulations against animals on naval vessels.

2000s – Gold Handprints
Fact: Kazakhstan's President Nursultan Nazarbayev had his handprints cast in gold and installed atop a tower so visitors could press their palms into them for luck.

1865 – Inauguration Hangover
Fact: Vice President Andrew Johnson showed up drunk to his inauguration, slurred his speech, and had to be helped off stage by President Lincoln.

1980 – $3 Million Wedding
Fact: Haitian President Jean-Claude Duvalier spent $3 million of public money on his wedding—while most of his country lived in poverty.

2016 – Paper Puzzle Presidency
Fact: President Donald Trump had a habit of tearing up official documents, so staff were tasked with taping them back together to comply with preservation laws.

1880s – Pants for Every Occasion
Fact: President Chester A. Arthur owned over 80 pairs of pants and changed outfits several times a day—earning the nickname "Elegant Arthur."

2011 – Presidential Rap Debut

Fact: Uganda's President Yoweri Museveni dropped a rap song titled "You Want Another Rap?" during his re-election campaign. It went viral.

2017 – Viral Victory Dance

Fact: Former Liberian President Ellen Johnson Sirleaf broke into a spontaneous victory dance after winning a $5 million leadership prize—unaware she was still on camera.

Present Day – Golden Garage Goals

Fact: Sultan Hassanal Bolkiah of Brunei owns over 7,000 luxury cars—some with gold hubcaps—and rotates them regularly to keep them running smoothly.

1970s – Golf Legend (Sort Of)

Fact: Philippine dictator Ferdinand Marcos claimed he was the best golfer in the world. State media reported he scored multiple holes-in-one every game.

Present Day – The Granddad President

Fact: President John Tyler (1790–1862) fathered 15 children. As of 2023, one of his grandsons was still alive—nearly 160 years after his death.

1980s – Jedi Council Meetings

Fact: Nicaraguan President Daniel Ortega made his cabinet watch *Star Wars* movies before meetings, claiming they offered insights into defeating U.S. imperialism.

2000   The Real Burger King

Fact: North Korea's Kim Jong-il claimed he invented the hamburger—describing it as "double bread with meat"—and offered it as a solution to national hunger.

Early 2000s – Romance Novelist-in-Chief

Fact: Saddam Hussein moonlighted as a romance novelist. His books were published under pen names and filled with propaganda disguised as passionate drama.

1960s – Dressed to Scare
Fact: Haitian President François Duvalier dressed like the Vodou spirit of death, Baron Samedi, to terrify his enemies and build a supernatural reputation.

1929–1933 – Stealth President
Fact: President Herbert Hoover hated seeing staff. White House employees were ordered to hide behind curtains or furniture whenever he entered a room.

1960s – Magical Fishing Ban
Fact: Guinea's President Ahmed Sékou Touré banned river fishing, believing the fish were magical spirits. Locals were warned that catching them would bring misfortune.

2015 – Gollum Lawsuit
Fact: Turkish President Recep Tayyip Erdoğan sued people for comparing him to Gollum. A Turkish court convened experts to analyze whether Gollum was actually insulting.

1877–1881 – Lemonade Lucy's Husband
Fact: President Rutherford B. Hayes banned alcohol from White House events, influenced by his teetotaler wife, "Lemonade Lucy"—though he quietly drank in private.

1970s – Lifted by Legends
Fact: Kenyan President Jomo Kenyatta had four men carry him in a chair for even short strolls, calling it "tradition." Spoiler: it wasn't.

1980 – Six-Hour Chant Ceremony
Fact: Somali President Siad Barre once forced schoolchildren to chant his name for six hours straight during a state ceremony under the scorching sun.

1872 – Galloping Ticket
Fact: Ulysses S. Grant, while president, was fined $20 for speeding on horseback through Washington D.C. He paid the fine without pulling rank.

1985 – Lucky Currency
Fact: Burma's leader Ne Win issued currency in weird denominations like 45 and 90 kyat because his astrologer told him numbers divisible by 9 would help him live longer.

1960s – Presidential Magic Man
Fact: Ghana's President Kwame Nkrumah kept a personal magician on the payroll. His job? Perform miracles in villages before Nkrumah's arrival to enhance his mystical aura.

1970s–80s – The Waving Handkerchief
Fact: Zambia's Kenneth Kaunda was known for waving a white handkerchief during speeches. It caught on so much that thousands of supporters waved their own back.

1977 – Throne of Gold
Fact: Central African Republic's Emperor Bokassa spent $20 million—nearly a quarter of the national budget—on a golden throne and Napoleon-style coronation.

1960s – Pre-Caught Fishing Films
Fact: Spanish dictator Francisco Franco starred in fishing documentaries… but with a twist. Staff pre-caught the fish to ensure he always looked like a master angler.

2010 – Shoe Denial
Fact: Sudan's President Omar al-Bashir was hit by a shoe thrown by a journalist. Though caught on video, he publicly denied the incident ever happened.

WWII Era – Trains Over Planes
Fact: Joseph Stalin hated flying. Instead, he traveled by heavily armored train complete with a movie room—where he screened his favorite cowboy flicks.

1900s – Obstacle Course Roosevelt
Fact: Theodore Roosevelt challenged guests to race across the White

House lawn in a straight line—regardless of obstacles like bushes, fences, or fountains.

1970s – Ferraris in the Dirt
Fact: Haiti's Baby Doc Duvalier collected Ferraris during the 1970s—even though Haiti had less than 10 miles of paved roads.

1970s – Santa Claus Exemption
Fact: Turkmenistan's Saparmurat Niyazov banned beards for being unhygienic… except for Santa, who was granted a beard pass each December.

1980s – No Flash Photography, Ever
Fact: Panama's Manuel Noriega was convinced flash photography could be used in voodoo spells. He constantly dodged cameras and refused photos during speeches.

1880s – Bilingual Showoff
Fact: President James Garfield could write Latin with one hand and Greek with the other at the same time. Because who doesn't want a multilingual party trick?

1970s–80s – Star-Crossed Diplomacy
Fact: Indonesia's Suharto refused meetings with foreign leaders if their star signs didn't match his. He even had an astrologer rearrange his diplomatic calendar.

2009 – The Missing Tiger
Fact: Ramzan Kadyrov, leader of Chechnya, lost his pet tiger cub in 2009. He locked down an entire city until it was found hiding in a neighbor's shed.

1960s – Wall Vision
Fact: "Papa Doc" Duvalier of Haiti spread rumors that he could see through walls and read minds—claims boosted by his secret police to maintain an aura of fear.

2003 – Divine Bank Account
Fact: Equatorial Guinea's Teodoro Obiang claimed he could speak directly

to God and was entrusted by Him to personally manage the country's oil wealth.

2011 – Presidential Fan Club

Fact: Russia's Dmitry Medvedev was such a fan of Deep Purple that he hosted a private concert—on the government's dime—and required officials to fake knowing the lyrics.

🚽 Flush-Worthy Firsts: Presidential Edition

History remembers the first to lead, the first to sign treaties, and the first to step on the moon... but these? These are presidential "firsts" you definitely didn't learn in school.

1913 – First President to Get Stuck in a Bathtub

William Howard Taft

Big man, small tub. After the infamous incident, he commissioned a custom-sized bathtub big enough for four average-sized men. Because presidential dignity has dimensions.

2000 – First (and Only) President to Resign via Fax

Alberto Fujimori

From Japan, no less. Who needs Air Force One when you have OfficeMax?

2007 – First President to Host an Eight-Hour Talk Show

Hugo Chávez

His TV program *Aló Presidente* was part variety show, part political speech, part musical performance. No intermissions. Ever.

1920s – First President to Lose His China in a Poker Game

Warren G. Harding

He bet the White House's official dinnerware. Spoiler: he didn't win.

1975 – First to Challenge Another Country to a Boxing Match

Idi Amin

Forget war—he invited Tanzania's president to settle things in the ring. Float like a dictator, sting like diplomacy?

3. Unbelievable Fiascos

37–41 CE – Caligula vs. the Ocean
Fact: Roman Emperor Caligula once declared war on Neptune. He had his army stab the waves and gather seashells, calling them the "spoils of war."

1919 – The Great Molasses Flood
Fact: In Boston, a massive molasses tank burst, sending a 35 mph wave through the streets. It killed 21 people and injured over 100 in one of history's stickiest disasters.

1518 – The Dancing Plague
Fact: In Strasbourg, dozens of people danced non-stop for days. The bizarre outbreak led to exhaustion—and even death—for some participants.

1807 – Napoleon's Bunny Beatdown
Fact: Napoleon planned a rabbit hunt for his men, but the bunnies turned the tables—swarming and chasing him off the field.

1920s–1933 – The Poisoned Booze Plan
Fact: During Prohibition, U.S. officials poisoned industrial alcohol to curb

illegal drinking. Bootleggers kept selling it anyway—causing thousands of deaths.

Early 1700s – The Potsdam Giants
Fact: King Frederick William I of Prussia created a regiment of towering soldiers. He was obsessed with their height and paraded them like prized collectibles.

Ancient Egypt – Human Flytraps
Fact: To keep flies away from the pharaoh, servants were smeared in honey so the insects would swarm them instead. Royal protection was a sticky business.

Victorian Era – Hairy Mourning Jewelry
Fact: Mourning got personal in the Victorian era—people wore intricate jewelry made from the actual hair of their dead loved ones.

1967 – Harold Holt Disappears
Fact: Australian Prime Minister Harold Holt went for a swim and vanished forever. Australia later honored him by naming... a swimming pool after him.

1233 – Papal War on Cats
Fact: Pope Gregory IX linked cats to devil worship, sparking mass exterminations. With fewer cats around, rats thrived—and the Black Death followed a century later.

1700s – The Potato Scam That Worked
Fact: King Frederick the Great wanted Prussians to eat potatoes. So he planted a guarded "royal" field to spark curiosity. Locals stole the crop—just as he hoped.

1915–1955 – The Man Who Never Slept
Fact: Hungarian soldier Paul Kern was shot in the head in WWI and never slept again. He lived 40 years without rest, baffling every doctor who examined him.

1590s – The Moose Who Drank Too Much
Fact: Danish astronomer Tycho Brahe owned a tame moose that loved

beer. At a party, the drunk moose fell down some stairs and died—ending a very odd friendship.

1726 – Rabbit Birth Hoax

Fact: Mary Toft tricked English doctors into believing she gave birth to rabbits. Her secret? Sneaking dead rabbits inside herself and staging dramatic "deliveries."

1920s – Petroleum Jelly Presidency

Fact: President Calvin Coolidge liked to eat breakfast in bed... while having his scalp rubbed with petroleum jelly. Leadership, his way.

1325 – War Over a Bucket

Fact: A war broke out between Modena and Bologna over a stolen wooden bucket. More than 2,000 died. The bucket? Still proudly displayed in Modena today.

1096 – Oxford Predates Algebra

Fact: Oxford University was already teaching students in 1096—nearly a full century before algebra even made its way to Europe.

Mid-1800s – The Fasting Girl Craze

Fact: Victorian England saw a bizarre trend: "fasting girl" exhibitions. These young women claimed to survive without food, insisting they lived only on air and sunlight. Crowds came to marvel—and debate whether it was a miracle or a lie.

1739 – War Of Jenkins' Ear

Fact: The conflict between Britain and Spain broke out all because a Spanish coast guard officer had cut off British sailor Robert Jenkins' ear eight years earlier—and people hadn't forgotten.

Mid-1700s – 15,000 Dresses Of Empress Elizabeth

Fact: Russian Empress Elizabeth had a taste for luxury like no other. During her reign, she owned more than 15,000 dresses—and never wore the same one twice.

1600s – Coffee Gets Papal Approval

Fact: When coffee first arrived in Europe, not everyone welcomed it. Some clergy denounced it as "the devil's drink." But Pope Clement VIII gave it a try, liked it, and gave it his official blessing—changing coffee's fate forever.

1698 – Beard Tax In Russia
Fact: Peter the Great launched an unusual campaign to modernize his country. He imposed a tax on beards and made men carry a "beard token" to prove they had paid up.

1911 – Mona Lisa Heist
Fact: A Parisian handyman named Vincenzo Peruggia pulled off one of history's boldest art heists. He hid inside the Louvre overnight, then calmly walked out the next morning with the Mona Lisa tucked under his coat.

1587 – Elbow Tea Party
Fact: Japanese warlord Toyotomi Hideyoshi threw a tea party unlike any other. Guests had to search for tea cups buried in the dirt—using only their elbows.

1940s – Franco: Caudillo Of Fashion
Fact: Spanish dictator Francisco Franco made a surprising appearance in women's magazines, where he was advertised as the "Caudillo of fashion," complete with photos modeling various outfits.

1700s – Louis Xiv's Bed Collection
Fact: During his long reign, King Louis XIV of France reportedly had 413 beds spread throughout his palaces.

1826 – Founding Fathers' Final Act
Fact: Thomas Jefferson and John Adams, once bitter rivals and later old friends, both passed away on July 4th, 1826—exactly 50 years after they helped shape American independence.

180–192 Ce – Commodus The "Hercules"
Fact: Roman Emperor Commodus believed he was the reincarnation of Hercules. Dressed in costume, he would enter the Colosseum and beat people to death with a club.

Cold War – Operation Acoustic Kitty

Fact: The CIA launched a $20 million project to turn cats into spies by implanting microphones in them. The first cat agent didn't make it past its first mission—it was hit by a taxi.

1974 – The Writer's Block Paper

Fact: The Journal of Applied Behavior Analysis published an unusual academic paper titled "The Unsuccessful Self-Treatment of a Case of 'Writer's Block.'" The entire article? Blank pages.

1380–1422 – The Glass King

Fact: King Charles VI of France ruled while convinced he was made of glass. He feared he might shatter at any moment and wore reinforced clothing for protection.

Ancient Rome – Flamingo Tongue Delicacy

Fact: Flamingo tongues weren't just food—they were considered a high-end delicacy, served at elite Roman banquets.

1896 – The Shortest War Ever

Fact: The shortest war in recorded history took place between Britain and Zanzibar on August 27, 1896. It lasted just 38 minutes.

1500s–1800s – Royal Bathroom Assistant

Fact: English royalty had a prestigious position called the "Groom of the Stool." The job? Helping the king use the toilet—and even wiping his bottom.

Wwii – Carrots And Night Vision

Fact: British intelligence spread a clever rumor that their snipers could see in the dark because they ate a lot of carrots. In truth, it was a cover-up to hide radar technology.

Early 1800s – Byron's Dorm Bear

Fact: Poet Lord Byron bypassed Cambridge University's "no dogs" policy by keeping a pet bear in his dorm room instead.

1550 Bce – Crocodile Dung Contraception
Fact: Ancient Egyptian women used crocodile dung as contraception. It was as unpleasant as it sounds—but believed to work.

13th Century – Genghis Khan's Carbon Footprint
Fact: Genghis Khan's devastating conquests reduced global population so drastically that around 700 million tons of carbon were removed from the atmosphere—cooling the planet.

1960s – Lbj's Vietnam Justification
Fact: When President Lyndon B. Johnson was asked why the U.S. was in Vietnam, he unzipped his pants, pulled out his genitals, and declared, "This is why."

218–222 CE – SNAKE WARFARE IN ROME
Fact: Roman Emperor Elagabalus amused himself by releasing venomous snakes into crowds during public events. It was as chaotic and dangerous as it sounds.

1942–1945 – Hitler's Nephew Fights Back
Fact: During World War II, Adolf Hitler's own nephew, William Hitler, served in the U.S. Navy—fighting against his infamous uncle.

1930s–1940s – Stalin Erases History
Fact: Soviet leader Joseph Stalin literally edited people out of history. When someone fell out of favor, they were removed from official photos—as if they had never existed.

1672 – Cannibal Revenge In The Netherlands
Fact: After Dutch Prime Minister Johan de Witt and his brother were killed by a mob, things took a gruesome turn—the angry crowd allegedly ate parts of their bodies in revenge.

1808 – Executing A Spy Elephant
Fact: During the Napoleonic Wars, the Spanish town of Cartagena executed a French elephant, believing it was a spy. No one questioned how an elephant could report back to Napoleon.

65 Ce – Nero Marries A Boy
Fact: Roman Emperor Nero missed his late wife so much that he castrated a young boy who resembled her, married him, and made everyone treat the boy as his empress.

1700s – Louis Xiv, King Of Rare Baths
Fact: King Louis XIV of France ruled for over 70 years—but reportedly only bathed three times in his entire life. Royal hygiene wasn't exactly majestic.

1750s – Franklin's Strange Symphony
Fact: Benjamin Franklin invented an instrument called the glass armonica, made of spinning glass bowls. It was so eerie, both Mozart and Beethoven wrote music for it.

1932–1972 – The Tuskegee Experiment
Fact: For 40 years, the U.S. government misled Black men into thinking they were being treated for "bad blood." In truth, doctors were secretly studying the effects of untreated syphilis.

Ancient Rome – Urine For Everything
Fact: Urine was a hot commodity in Ancient Rome. It was collected to clean clothes, tan leather, and even whiten teeth—thanks to its ammonia content.

Wwii – Bat Bomb Fail
Fact: The U.S. military tried to weaponize bats by strapping tiny bombs to them, hoping they'd roost in enemy buildings before exploding. Spoiler: it didn't work.

1386 – A Pig On Trial
Fact: In medieval France, a pig was tried in court for killing a child—and was sentenced to death by hanging. Justice was blind... and bizarre.

1430s – Pirate Queen Of Revenge
Fact: Jeanne de Clisson turned pirate after her husband's execution by the French crown. She hunted down French nobles and personally beheaded them with an axe.

1925 – Eiffel Tower For Sale (Twice!)
Fact: Con artist Victor Lustig pulled off one of history's boldest scams—he "sold" the Eiffel Tower not once, but twice, fooling scrap metal dealers each time.

1494 – Ban On Pointy Shoes
Fact: Maximilian I banned pointed shoes in Switzerland, calling them impractical and ridiculous. Medieval fashion police, activate!

1930s – Tesla's Pigeon Love
Fact: Nikola Tesla claimed he was in love with a pigeon in New York City. He said she loved him too—and when she died, a light from her eyes was "more powerful than anything I ever created."

1977 – Guillotine Vs. Star Wars
Fact: France was still executing people by guillotine when Star Wars premiered in 1977. The final beheading and the film's release happened the same year.

1726 – Peter The Wild Boy
Fact: King George I of England adopted a feral boy found in a German forest and brought him to court as a "human pet." He never learned to speak but enjoyed raw vegetables.

Cleopatra Vs. The Iphone
Fact: Cleopatra lived closer in time to the iPhone (2007) than to the building of the Great Pyramid (2560 BCE). Time flies when you're a queen.

1805   Monkey Spy Trial
Fact: A monkey captured in South America was tried and convicted in England as a French spy during the Napoleonic Wars. Verdict: guilty, and bananas.

1929–1933 – Hoover's Hide-And-Seek
Fact: President Herbert Hoover hated small talk so much that his staff would literally hide behind furniture to avoid him as he walked by.

1861 – Elephants For Lincoln
Fact: The King of Siam (now Thailand) offered Abraham Lincoln a gift of

war elephants during the American Civil War. Lincoln politely declined—no room in the Union Army for a stampede.

14th Century – Cats Vs. Monks
Fact: Medieval monks often complained about cats walking across their freshly written manuscripts—leaving behind permanent paw prints in ink. Furry vandalism at its finest.

1981 – Ostrich Vs. Johnny Cash
Fact: Music legend Johnny Cash was nearly killed by an angry ostrich on his farm. He fought it off using a stick, surviving with broken ribs and a giant story.

1760s – Mummified Sales Tactic
Fact: A London cigar shop once displayed what looked like a wooden statue of a Native American. Turns out, it was an actual mummified body on display for decades.

Roman Times – Salt For Salary
Fact: Roman soldiers were sometimes paid in salt. The Latin word for "salary" even comes from salarium—a salt allowance. That's one salty paycheck.

2025 – Still At War (Technically)
Fact: Japan and Russia still haven't officially ended World War II due to a lingering dispute over a few tiny islands. Talk about holding a grudge.

1930s – Churchill's Nude Portrait
Fact: A young Winston Churchill once posed nude for a painting. Years later, he insisted it be called "nude" and not "naked," for the sake of dignity.

1816 – Frankenstein's Rainy Birth
Fact: During the "Year Without a Summer" caused by a volcanic eruption, Mary Shelley wrote Frankenstein while stuck indoors. Sometimes boredom sparks brilliance.

1761 – Army Vs. Itself
Fact: The Austrian army once accidentally attacked itself during the Battle

of Karánsebes, losing 10,000 men due to drunken confusion and friendly fire.

17th Century – Leech Face-Lifts
Fact: English women once applied leeches to their faces to achieve paler skin. The fashionable look? Light complexion—with a hint of blood loss.

2012 – Avoiding The Draft With 24 Eggs
Fact: In South Korea, some men intentionally gained weight to dodge military service. One man reportedly ate 24 eggs, over 3kg of pork, and protein powder to balloon up to 154kg. That's dedication… or indigestion.

Roman Times – Mouse Brain Toothpaste
Fact: Ancient Romans used crushed mouse brains to clean their teeth. Minty fresh? Not quite. Rodent rinse, anyone?

1970s – Ford's Multitasking Myth
Fact: President Gerald Ford was mocked for supposedly not being able to walk and chew gum at the same time. The press even coined it as a national metaphor for clumsiness.

1903 – Elephant Vs. Electricity
Fact: Thomas Edison electrocuted an elephant named Topsy to discredit rival Nikola Tesla's alternating current. It didn't end well—for the elephant or Edison's reputation.

1839 – Victoria Popped The Question
Fact: Queen Victoria broke tradition by proposing to Prince Albert herself. In royal romance, sometimes the crown takes charge.

1911 – Jack Daniel's Deadly Kick
Fact: Jack Daniel, founder of the famous whiskey brand, died from a foot infection… after angrily kicking his office safe. That's one fatal temper tantrum.

1096 Vs. 1428 – Oxford Beats The Aztecs
Fact: Oxford University was already teaching students long before the Aztec Empire even existed. The ivy was ancient before pyramids rose in Mexico.

13th Century – Tall, Milky Warriors
Fact: Genghis Khan's troops were taller than average thanks to a protein-packed diet rich in meat and fermented milk. No growth hormones needed.

Cleopatra – Not Egyptian
Fact: Despite ruling Egypt, Cleopatra was actually of Greek descent. Her family, the Ptolemies, were Macedonian imports.

1969–1974 – BOWLING NIXON
Fact: President Richard Nixon loved bowling so much, he had a one-lane alley installed in the White House. Strike while the presidency's hot.

1775 – The Ride That Didn't Finish
Fact: Paul Revere's famous midnight ride to warn of the British? He didn't finish it. He was detained, and two other riders carried the message through. Revere just had the better PR.

Early 1900s – Tobacco Butt Cpr
Fact: People once believed that blowing tobacco smoke into the rectum of a drowning person could revive them. Lifesaving was never so smoky... or awkward.

11th Century – Bearded Fame
Fact: Viking king Harald Hardrada had a beard so impressive, it had its own name. Sadly, the name has been lost—along with any hope of beard envy survival.

Early 1900s – Cereal Vs. Sin
Fact: Dr. John Harvey Kellogg invented corn flakes to suppress sexual urges. He believed bland food would kill the desire to, well... self-snack.

Ancient Rome – Sponge On A Stick
Fact: Wealthy Romans cleaned themselves with a sea sponge attached to a stick. They soaked it in salt water and reused it. Suddenly, modern toilet paper feels luxurious.

1955 – Einstein's Eyes In A Box
Fact: After Einstein's death, his eyes were removed and stored in a New Jersey safe deposit box. Visionary, even postmortem.

Ancient Rome – Urine For Teeth
Fact: Romans used urine to whiten their teeth. Why? The ammonia helped. Still gross? Absolutely.

1915 – The Chaplin Look-Alike Fail
Fact: Charlie Chaplin once entered a Charlie Chaplin look-alike contest—and lost. He didn't even make the finals.

63 BCE – Too Immune to Die
Fact: King Mithridates VI took small doses of poison daily to build immunity. It worked—so well, he couldn't kill himself with poison later and had to ask a soldier for help.

1912 – Coat-Parachute Catastrophe
Fact: Tailor Franz Reichelt tested his parachute coat by jumping off the Eiffel Tower. It didn't open. Fashion failed—fatally.

Aztec Times – Chocolate As Currency
Fact: The Aztecs used cacao beans as money. So technically, they could eat their savings—but hopefully not during inflation.

955–964 Ce – The Wild Pope
Fact: Pope John XII turned the Vatican into a brothel and was allegedly killed by a jealous husband while caught in the act. Divine judgment came quickly.

1771 – Death By Dessert
Fact: Swedish King Adolf Frederick died after a massive meal that included lobster, caviar, and 14 servings of dessert. It was a sweet end—literally.

Second Punic War – Elephants With Blades
Fact: Hannibal's war elephants went into battle with swords strapped to their tusks. That's one way to bring trunk-based terror.

1800s – Wake-Up Knockers
Fact: Before alarm clocks, "knocker-uppers" used long sticks to tap windows and wake people up for work. Today, we just call that an annoying neighbor.

1952 – Einstein For President?
Fact: Albert Einstein was offered the presidency of Israel. He declined, saying he lacked the natural aptitude and experience to deal with people.

1912 – The Drunken Titanic Survivor
Fact: One Titanic fireman drank so much before the ship sank that the alcohol may have helped him survive the freezing waters. A toast to unlikely flotation.

1534 – Death By Medicine
Fact: When Pope Clement VII died, his doctors were put on trial—accused of killing him with their treatments. Talk about fatal malpractice.

1970s – Vodka In Space
Fact: A translation mix-up reportedly sent Russian astronauts to space with vodka instead of rum. Cheers to cosmic confusion.

1916 – Rasputin's Epic End
Fact: Rasputin was poisoned, shot, beaten, and still didn't die—until he was drowned in a frozen river. If you want someone gone, don't pick a mystic monk.

1173–1372 – Pisa's Tilted Project
Fact: The Leaning Tower of Pisa began tilting early in construction. Builders noticed… and just kept building. Gravity, schmavity.

Medieval Europe – Buttering The Wound
Fact: Before antiseptics, people rubbed butter on cuts, believing it would help them heal. Unless you were toast, it probably didn't.

1918 – The Soldier Who Spared Hitler
Fact: A British soldier encountered a wounded German in WWI and let him go. That man? Adolf Hitler. History had one hell of a plot twist coming.

1960s – Nasa's Pricey Pen
Fact: NASA spent millions designing a space pen. The Soviets just used pencils. Sometimes, the best solution costs 12 cents.

1955 – Einstein's Brain Heist
Fact: After Einstein's death, the doctor removed his brain—without permission—and kept it for "research." That's not science, that's souvenir collecting.

1894 – Radio Has No Future
Fact: Lord Kelvin, a top physicist, once said radio had no future. So much for being tuned in.

Marie Antoinette – Misquoted Queen
Fact: "Let them eat cake" wasn't said by Marie Antoinette. The line was falsely pinned on her decades before she even became queen. She lost her head over bad PR.

1300–1521 – Worshipping Turkeys
Fact: The Aztecs didn't just eat turkeys—they worshipped them. Thanksgiving must've been awkward.

1912 – Boozy Buoyancy Part Ii
Fact: Titanic's chief baker Charles Joughin survived the icy waters by drinking heavily before the ship sank. Alcohol: 1, Hypothermia: 0.

1714–1727 – The King Who Couldn't Speak English
Fact: King George I of England barely spoke English. Not ideal for a king of England, but great for awkward silences.

1840s – The Doctor Who Was Too Clean
Fact: Dr. Ignaz Semmelweis suggested doctors wash their hands before delivering babies. He was mocked, locked in an asylum, and beaten to death. Today, ignoring new ideas is called the "Semmelweis Reflex."

1782 – Mozart's Rear-End Anthem
Fact: Mozart composed a tune called Leck mich im Arsch, which translates to "Lick me in the rear." It was less symphony, more sass.

World War I – Renaming Diseases
Fact: To distance themselves from Germany during WWI, Americans renamed "German measles" to "Liberty measles." Take that, germs.

1930s – Fashion In A Flour Sack
Fact: During the Great Depression, families made clothes from food sacks. In response, flour companies started printing colorful patterns on them. That's called sewing with style.

12th Century – Animals On Trial
Fact: In medieval England, animals were put on trial like humans. They even had legal representation. Court was literally for the birds.

1825–1829 – The Presidential Dip
Fact: President John Quincy Adams started his mornings with a naked swim in the Potomac River. That's one way to lead with confidence.

1600s – Potato Panic
Fact: When potatoes first arrived in Europe, some believed they caused leprosy. Clearly, hash browns hadn't been invented yet.

Viking Age – Skull Chalices
Fact: Vikings allegedly drank from the skulls of their enemies. It really put the "metal" in mealtime.

Victorian England – Calf Confidence
Fact: In the 1800s, some men wore fake calves inside their socks to look more muscular. Step aside, protein powder.

Aztec Wordplay – Avocado Origins
Fact: The word "avocado" comes from the Aztec ahuacatl, meaning "testicle." Suddenly, guacamole feels more personal.

958–986 – The Bluetooth Tooth
Fact: Viking king Harald "Bluetooth" got his nickname from a rotten, darkened tooth. Today's wireless tech is named after his dental disaster. Call it cavity-powered connection.

1830s – Darwin Dined Differently
Fact: Charles Darwin didn't just study exotic animals on his voyage—he ate them too. Science was delicious.

1945 – Miracle Mike, The Headless Chicken
Fact: A chicken named Mike survived for 18 months after being decapitated. He became a celebrity—though his interviews were understandably quiet.

Victorian Era – Posing With The Departed
Fact: It was trendy to take photos with dead relatives, propping them up to look alive. Talk about stiff competition in family portraits.

18th Century – Asylum Spectacles
Fact: Visiting mental asylums was considered entertainment in 1700s England. People paid to gawk at the patients like it was a zoo.

1135 – The Eel That Killed A King
Fact: King Henry I of England died after ignoring his doctor's advice and eating too many lampreys. That's death by seafood stubbornness.

Early 20th Century – The Man Who Wrecked The World
Fact: Thomas Midgley Jr. invented both leaded gasoline and CFCs. His work caused more damage to the environment than nearly anyone else in history. Not all geniuses are blessings.

3000 Bce – Ancient Diabetes Diagnosis
Fact: Mesopotamian doctors tasted their patients' urine to check for diabetes. If it was sweet, they knew something was wrong. Definitely not the best part of the job.

1920 – Love, Actually (Complicated)
Fact: A man in New Orleans couldn't choose between his three mistresses, so he left his house to one of them—in his will. Surprise inheritance by elimination!

1974 – 29 Years In The Jungle
Fact: Japanese soldier Hiroo Onoda surrendered in 1974, having hidden in the jungle since WWII, unaware the war had ended. Now that's commitment.

1770s – Jefferson's Chair Swivel
Fact: Thomas Jefferson invented the swivel chair in the 1770s. It's the unsung hero behind every office daydream.

Aztec Era – Plenty Of... What Now?
Fact: Emperor Montezuma's nephew was named Cuitláhuac—meaning "plenty of excrement." Royal names weren't always majestic.

1930 – The Building That Moved... While Working
Fact: The Indiana Bell Telephone Company rotated an entire 8-story building 90 degrees while employees kept working inside. Now that's multitasking.

180–192 Ce – Gladiator Emperor
Fact: Roman Emperor Commodus staged gladiator fights—against injured soldiers and amputees. Safe to say the odds were in his favor.

1830s – Ketchup As Medicine
Fact: Ketchup was once sold as a cure for diarrhea, indigestion, and jaundice. Who knew burgers were medicinal?

Early 1900s – Heroin For Your Cough
Fact: Heroin was marketed as a non-addictive alternative to morphine and used as a cough suppressant. Spoiler: it was addictive.

1860s – Lincoln's Surprising Voice
Fact: Despite Hollywood's portrayals, Abraham Lincoln had a high-pitched voice. So much for booming presidential authority.

17th Century – Stylish Scars
Fact: Smallpox survivors in Europe used velvet patches shaped like stars and hearts to cover their scars. Fashion from affliction.

Ancient Egypt – Head Perfume
Fact: Egyptians wore scented fat cones on their heads during events. As the night went on, they melted and released fragrance. Talk about a slow burn.

Ancient Sparta – No Room For Weakness
Fact: Spartan newborns were inspected for strength. Those who didn't pass were left to die on cliffs. Brutal beginnings.

279 Bce – Death By Laughter
Fact: Greek philosopher Chrysippus is said to have died laughing after watching a donkey eat his figs. The donkey lived; the philosopher didn't.

Victorian Era – Poisonous Beauty
Fact: Women used arsenic to lighten their skin, chasing a deadly glow. Beauty standards were... lethal.

15th Century – The Erotic Pope
Fact: Before becoming Pope Pius II, Aeneas Silvius Piccolomini penned a steamy novel titled The Tale of Two Lovers. Amen?

17th Century – The Birth Of Orange Carrots
Fact: Carrots weren't always orange—they were bred that way in the Netherlands to honor William of Orange. Yes, patriotism turned produce.

39 Ce – A Horse In The Senate
Fact: Emperor Caligula appointed his horse as a Roman senator. At least it couldn't filibuster.

1861 – A Gun To End Wars?
Fact: Richard Gatling invented the machine gun hoping it would make wars so deadly, no one would fight them. History disagreed.

Medieval Era – Hot Sand Training
Fact: Knights trained for battle by pouring hot sand into their armor. Because chafing builds character.

1173–1372 – Pisa's Tilted Plan
Fact: The Leaning Tower of Pisa started tilting during construction, but builders kept going. "It's not a flaw—it's flair."

17th Century – Brow Pets
Fact: Women in England glued live mice to their eyebrows for fashion. That trend thankfully died—unlike the mice.

1692 – Witchcraft... Dog?

Fact: During the Salem Witch Trials, a dog was executed for witchcraft. Even good boys weren't safe.

Medieval Europe – Buttering The Wound

Fact: Before antibiotics, people believed rubbing butter on wounds would help them heal. It didn't—unless you were toast.

Einstein Myth

Fact: Despite the rumors, Einstein never failed math. He actually mastered calculus by age 15. Sorry, internet memes.

Vikings – Horned Helmet Myth

Fact: Vikings likely never wore horned helmets. That image came from 19th-century opera costumes, not battlefields.

1932 – The Great Emu War

Fact: Australia launched a military campaign against emus using machine guns. The emus won.

Ancient Egypt – Buggy Makeup

Fact: Egyptians used crushed bugs and minerals for eyeliner. Beauty was pain—and insects.

1934–1963 – Alcatraz Hot Showers

Fact: Inmates at Alcatraz got hot showers—not as a luxury, but to stop them from adapting to cold water and escaping.

🚽 Fiasco Fallout – A Blunder Blitz!

Welcome to your Bathroom Fiasco Fallout Quiz! Five unbelievable fails, only one true gem in each. Can you spot the real misstep? Don't slip up!

#1 Which U.S. city was once flooded... by molasses?

☐ A) Philadelphia   ☐ C) Boston

☐ B) Chicago   ☐ D) New Orleans

#2 What did Roman Emperor Caligula "declare war" on?

- [ ] A) The moon
- [ ] C) The sea
- [ ] B) His sandals
- [ ] D) Cabbage

#3 How did Napoleon's rabbit hunt end?

- [ ] A) All rabbits escaped
- [ ] C) Rabbits attacked him
- [ ] B) Napoleon was bitten
- [ ] D) He fell asleep in the field

#4 What did a woman in 1726 pretend to give birth to?

- [ ] A) Rocks
- [ ] C) Rabbits
- [ ] B) Chickens
- [ ] D) Peasants

#5 What mysterious plague struck Strasbourg in 1518?

- [ ] A) Sneezing fits
- [ ] C) Laughter
- [ ] B) Public singing
- [ ] D) Dancing

Answers:

1 – C, 2 – C, 3 – C, 4 – C, 5 – D

4. Epic Failures In History

1969–1972 – Soviet N1 Rocket Explosions
Fact: The Soviet N1 rocket exploded four times, including once on the launchpad. One blast became the largest non-nuclear explosion in history and ended the USSR's hopes of reaching the moon.

1940 – Tacoma Narrows Bridge Collapse
Fact: Just four months after opening, the Tacoma Narrows Bridge twisted itself apart due to wind resonance. The footage is still shown in physics classes as a textbook disaster.

1920s – Thomas Midgley Jr.'s Toxic Legacy
Fact: Midgley created both leaded gasoline and CFCs—two inventions that damaged human health and the environment. He's been called history's most dangerous inventor.

1950s – The Ford Edsel Flop
Fact: Ford spent millions marketing the Edsel, only to have consumers hate its design. The company lost $350 million—about $3.4 billion today—on this automotive embarrassment.

1937 – Hindenburg Disaster
Fact: The Hindenburg exploded in just 36 seconds while landing, killing 36 people. The dramatic footage and the cry "Oh, the humanity!" ended the era of passenger airships.

1962 – Beatles Rejected by Decca Records
Fact: Decca Records passed on The Beatles, claiming guitar bands were out. That one decision may be the worst talent rejection in music history.

2000 – AOL-Time Warner Merger
Fact: The $165 billion AOL-Time Warner merger became a $200 billion disaster. The companies clashed, lost value, and Time Warner later called it "the worst deal of the century."

1912 – Titanic's 'Unsinkable' Sinking
Fact: Touted as unsinkable, the Titanic went down on its first voyage after hitting an iceberg. About 1,500 people died, and the world got a harsh lesson in hubris.

64 CE – Nero Fiddles as Rome Burns
Fact: Emperor Nero allegedly played music as Rome went up in flames. He later blamed the Christians, starting one of history's most infamous persecutions.

1976 – Swine Flu Vaccine Fiasco
Fact: The U.S. vaccinated 45 million people against swine flu, which never came. But the vaccine caused 450 cases of Guillain-Barré syndrome, creating a medical and PR disaster.

1961 – Bay of Pigs Invasion
Fact: The CIA-backed invasion of Cuba by anti-Castro exiles failed within three days. It embarrassed the U.S. and strengthened Fidel Castro's grip on power.

1930s–1940 – France's Maginot Line
Fact: France built a massive defensive wall to stop Germany, but in 1940 the Germans simply went around it through Belgium. Billions wasted on the wrong kind of protection.

1985 – Coca-Cola Launches New Coke
Fact: Coca-Cola replaced its classic soda with "New Coke," sparking nationwide backlash. Just 79 days later, they brought the original back, branding it "Coca-Cola Classic."

1812 – Napoleon's Russian Invasion
Fact: Napoleon marched 680,000 troops into Russia; only 27,000 returned. The brutal winter and scorched-earth strategy left his empire in tatters.

2000 – Blockbuster Rejects Netflix
Fact: Netflix offered to sell for $50 million, but Blockbuster laughed them off. By 2010, Blockbuster was bankrupt and Netflix was streaming its way to the top.

1588 – Spanish Armada Sinks
Fact: Spain sent 130 ships to conquer England, but half were sunk by storms and English forces. It was a turning point that ended Spain's naval dominance.

1999 – Excite Says "No Thanks" to Google
Fact: Google offered itself for $750,000, but Excite's CEO declined. Today, Google is worth over $1 trillion, and Excite is barely a footnote in tech history.

1937 – Soviet Census Suppressed
Fact: The Soviet census showed 8 million missing citizens. Stalin responded not by fixing the problem—but by executing the statisticians and hiding the results.

9 CE – Roman Defeat in Teutoburg Forest
Fact: Rome lost 20,000 soldiers to Germanic tribes due to arrogance and poor planning. The defeat permanently ended Roman expansion into northern Europe.

1975–2012 – Kodak's Missed Moment
Fact: Kodak invented the digital camera in 1975 but buried it to protect film sales. By the time they embraced digital, it was too late—and they went bankrupt.

1954 – Windscale Nuclear Disaster
Fact: A fire broke out at Britain's first nuclear reactor, but a faulty temperature sensor gave false readings. Radiation spread across Europe before it was stopped.

1720 – The South Sea Bubble
Fact: The South Sea Company's stock surged 1,000% before crashing entirely. Thousands lost their savings, and the scandal birthed the phrase "bubble burst."

1996 – McDonald's Arch Deluxe Flop
Fact: McDonald's spent $300 million promoting a "gourmet" burger for adults. Nobody wanted it, and it quickly became one of the biggest fast-food flops ever.

1999 – Mars Climate Orbiter Mishap
Fact: NASA lost a $327 million orbiter because one team used metric units and another used imperial. The spacecraft disintegrated in Mars' atmosphere.

1986 – Challenger Shuttle Disaster
Fact: Engineers warned of O-ring failure in cold weather, but NASA launched anyway. The shuttle exploded on live TV, killing all seven crew members.

1845–1852 – Irish Potato Famine
Fact: A million died in the famine while Ireland exported food to England. Poor policies made a natural disaster into a national tragedy.

2007 – Nokia's Smartphone Blindspot
Fact: Nokia dismissed the iPhone as a fad. Within five years, the company that once led the mobile world had lost it all.

1998 – Iridium Satellite Failure
Fact: Iridium launched 66 satellites for a $5 billion phone system, but no one wanted $3,000 phones. They went bankrupt in less than a year.

1842 – First Anglo-Afghan War Disaster
Fact: Of 16,000 British troops and civilians retreating from Kabul, only

one European made it out alive. It was one of history's most humiliating retreats.

1980s – Sony's Betamax Loses to VHS
Fact: Betamax had better quality, but VHS had longer recording and adult content. Consumers chose VHS, and Betamax faded into tech history.

1785 – Balloon Explosion Attempt
Fact: Jean-François Pilâtre de Rozier tried to cross the English Channel with a hydrogen balloon under a hot-air one. It exploded mid-air—no surprise there.

1994 – Quaker Oats Buys Snapple
Fact: Quaker Oats bought Snapple for $1.7 billion but didn't understand the brand. They sold it for just $300 million three years later.

1895 – The Navy's Rusty Rifle
Fact: The Navy's Lee rifle rusted in sea air and was hard to aim on moving ships. It sank faster than the sailors who used it.

1997–2008 – Yahoo's Tech Blunders
Fact: Yahoo passed on Google, Facebook, and even Microsoft's buyout offer. After all that, it sold for a mere $4.5 billion in 2017.

1958 – China's Sparrow Campaign
Fact: China killed sparrows to protect crops, but it backfired. Without birds, insects swarmed fields and helped trigger a deadly famine.

1908 – US Steel Rejects Reinforced Concrete
Fact: US Steel ignored a concrete innovation that competitors used to build skyscrapers. They stuck with old methods—and missed a construction revolution.

2001 – XFL Football Fumbles
Fact: Backed by WWE and NBC, the XFL launched with hype but flopped after one season. Poor quality and bad ratings ended it fast.

1200s – Easter Island Tree Massacre
Fact: Islanders cut down all their trees to move giant stone heads. No trees, no survival. Their civilization collapsed along with the forest.

2011 – Japan's Failed Flood Vault
Fact: Japan built a $1.5 billion underground vault to manage disasters, but forgot to seal ventilation shafts. It flooded during the 2011 tsunami.

1954 – Britain's Cracking Jetliners
Fact: The Comet jetliner had square windows that caused metal fatigue. Three planes broke apart mid-air, nearly ending the UK's aviation future.

1919 – The Great Molasses Flood
Fact: A molasses tank burst in Boston, unleashing a 15-foot wave at 35 mph. It killed 21 people and injured 150—sweet, but deadly.

1803 – The Louisiana Purchase
Fact: Napoleon sold 828,000 square miles of land to the U.S. for just $15 million. That's about 4 cents an acre—and one massive bargain.

1957 – The Ford Edsel
Fact: The Edsel's design was so odd it got nicknames like "toilet seat grille." It became Ford's most expensive and awkward flop.

1999 – Mars Polar Lander Crash
Fact: NASA engineers forgot to factor in vibrations. The probe shut off its engines too early and crashed—another Martian mission down the drain.

1788 – Britain's Rotten Navy
Fact: Shipworms ate through British ships' wooden hulls near Spithead. Warnings were ignored, and the fleet literally sank itself.

1930 – The R101 Airship Crash
Fact: Britain rushed the R101 into service to beat Germany. It crashed on its first international trip, killing 48 out of 54 aboard.

1867 – Alaska's Bargain Buy
Fact: The U.S. bought Alaska from Russia for $7.2 million. Seen as a frozen wasteland then, it later turned into a resource jackpot.

1943 – The USS Eldridge Teleportation Myth
Fact: Rumors claimed the ship vanished and reappeared during a Navy experiment. Some said crew members fused into the hull. Officially, it never happened.

2001 – Enron's Collapse
Fact: Enron collapsed in just 24 days after faking profits. It wiped out $74 billion in value and became a symbol of corporate fraud.

1943 – Bat Bombs Gone Wrong
Fact: The U.S. trained bats to carry firebombs. They escaped during testing—and accidentally burned down a U.S. airbase. Project canceled.

1968 – The Eternal Chicken Poop Fire
Fact: A farm in Arizona accidentally ignited 3,000 tons of chicken manure. It smoldered underground for 15 years, outlasting the business itself.

1980 – IBM's Billion-Dollar Mistake
Fact: IBM let Microsoft keep rights to MS-DOS. That one decision made Bill Gates a tech titan—and left IBM in the dust.

2007 – Boston LED Bomb Scare
Fact: An LED ad campaign caused a bomb scare in Boston. The city shut down, and the company paid $2 million in fines for cartoon paranoia.

1980s – GM's Robot Revolution Fails
Fact: GM spent $45 billion on factory robots. They couldn't install windshields properly and sometimes painted each other instead of the cars.

1961 – USS Forrestal Disaster
Fact: A rocket misfire sparked a deadly fire on the USS Forrestal, killing 134 sailors. It was the worst U.S. Navy accident since WWII.

2000 – The End of Concorde
Fact: After a crash caused by runway debris, the supersonic Concorde was grounded forever. Fast flight dreams faded with a fiery finale.

1999 – NASA's Unit Mix-Up
Fact: NASA lost a $125 million Mars probe because one team used inches and another used centimeters. A simple math mistake ended in flames.

2000s – The Dot-Com Disaster
Fact: Tech startups with no profits were worth billions. Then the bubble burst—like Pets.com, which collapsed in under a year.

1961 – Catch-22 Nearly Missed
Fact: Joseph Heller's now-classic *Catch-22* was released with just 7,500 copies. Publishers thought it wouldn't sell. Ten million readers proved otherwise.

2011 – Fukushima Disaster
Fact: A tsunami flooded Japan's Fukushima plant, knocking out power. The meltdown exposed flawed designs and sparked global nuclear fear.

1989 – Loma Prieta Earthquake
Fact: The San Francisco freeway collapsed during the quake, revealing the dangers of building heavy infrastructure on soft, unreinforced soil.

1986 – Challenger Explosion (Again!)
Fact: Despite warnings, NASA launched the Challenger in freezing weather. Faulty O-rings caused it to explode on live TV, killing all seven astronauts.

1878 – HMS Eurydice Sinks
Fact: The HMS Eurydice sailed into a storm with its gunports open. Water poured in, sinking the ship and killing 317 sailors. Talk about an avoidable tragedy.

1993 – Apple's Newton
Fact: Apple's Newton PDA had handwriting recognition so bad it turned "hello" into "hellop." It cost $100 million and became an expensive punchline.

1876 – Custer's Last Stand
Fact: General Custer attacked a massive Native American force and

refused reinforcements. His entire unit was wiped out. That's not brave—it's reckless.

1941 – The Yamato Battleship
Fact: Japan built the largest battleship ever—the Yamato—calling it unsinkable. U.S. planes sank it before it proved itself in battle. Oops.

2001 – Enron's Collapse
Fact: Enron faked profits, fooled Wall Street, and collapsed in just 24 days—erasing $70 billion and becoming the poster child for corporate fraud.

1903 – Iroquois Theatre Fire
Fact: Chicago's "fireproof" Iroquois Theatre had locked exits. When a fire broke out, 602 people died, triggering major safety reforms.

1970s – Schlitz Beer's Recipe Blunder
Fact: Schlitz tried to cut costs by changing its beer recipe. Fans hated it, sales tanked, and the company fizzled out after a century on top.

1912 – The Election That Split the Right
Fact: Teddy Roosevelt ran against his own party, splitting the Republican vote. Democrat Woodrow Wilson won with just 42%. Thanks, Bull Moose.

1975 – The DeLorean Disaster
Fact: The DeLorean looked futuristic but was slow, unreliable, and leaked in the rain. Only 9,000 were sold before the company crashed harder than its doors.

1958 – China's "Sparrow Campaign"
Fact: To save crops, China killed millions of sparrows. Without birds, insects took over—causing a famine that killed tens of millions. Nature fought back.

1962 – Beatles Rejected by Decca Records
Fact: Decca Records turned down The Beatles, saying "guitar groups are on the way out." It remains one of the worst talent decisions in music history.

1911 – Race to the South Pole
Fact: Robert Scott reached the South Pole in 1912, only to learn Roald Amundsen beat him there. On the return trip, Scott and his team perished.

1854 – The Charge of the Light Brigade
Fact: A miscommunication sent British cavalry charging into Russian cannons. Nearly half died in 20 minutes. Glorious? Maybe. Smart? Definitely not.

1980 – Miracle on Ice... For the U.S., a Disaster for the Soviets
Fact: The Soviet hockey team hadn't lost in 14 years—until a team of U.S. college players beat them at the 1980 Olympics. Total Soviet shock.

1943 – The Kassel Bombing Debacle
Fact: The U.S. 4th Bombardment Wing got separated from its fighter escorts and lost 43 of 96 bombers in a single raid—because of bad coordination.

2004 – Athens Olympics: Gold Medal in Overspending
Fact: Greece built extravagant stadiums for the 2004 Olympics. Most were abandoned, and the debt helped trigger a national financial crisis.

1998–2008 – Yahoo's Billion-Dollar Blunders
Fact: Yahoo turned down Google, Facebook, and a $44.6B buyout from Microsoft. By 2017, it sold for just $4.5B. That's a billion-dollar oops.

1929 – St. Valentine's Day Massacre
Fact: Al Capone's men killed seven gang rivals in broad daylight. The public was so horrified, it helped bring Prohibition closer to an end.

1999 – WebVan Delivers Bankruptcy
Fact: WebVan spent $1.2 billion on high-tech warehouses for online groceries—but no one was ready. The company went bankrupt within two years.

1854 – The Franklin Expedition's Frozen End
Fact: All 129 men on the Franklin Expedition died searching for the Northwest Passage. Many were likely poisoned by lead from their canned food.

1993 – Waco Siege Tragedy
Fact: A raid on the Branch Davidian compound ended in fire and death. Seventy-six people, including women and children, were killed in the blaze.

1995 – Sega Saturn's Not-So-Super Launch
Fact: Sega released the Saturn early, priced it high, and had few games. Sony and Nintendo dominated while Sega fumbled hard.

2007 – The Great Housing Crash
Fact: Risky home loans were sold as safe investments. When homeowners defaulted, the entire global economy nearly collapsed. Thanks, Wall Street.

1941 – Hitler's Icy Miscalculation
Fact: Hitler invaded the Soviet Union in winter with 3 million troops. He lost nearly 5 million. Turns out, snow beats tanks.

1518 – The Dancing Plague
Fact: In Strasbourg, hundreds danced uncontrollably for days—some to death. The "cure" back then? Even more dancing. Medical mystery meets medieval rave.

1990s – Motorola Misses the Message
Fact: Motorola dominated with flip phones but dismissed smartphones. One exec even mocked the iPhone. Apple laughed all the way to the bank.

1803 – Napoleon's Fire Sale
Fact: Napoleon sold the Louisiana Territory to the U.S. for $15 million. That land is now worth hundreds of billions. Whoops.

1917 – Halifax Boom
Fact: A ship full of explosives collided in Halifax harbor, causing the biggest non-nuclear blast in history. It killed 1,700 and flattened the city.

1975 – Cod Crisis Crunch
Fact: Arthur Treacher's Fish & Chips had 800 locations until cod prices soared during the Cod Wars. Without fish, customers bailed and the chain sank fast.

1959 – The Champagne Curse
Fact: At the USS Triton launch, the champagne bottle refused to break. Sailors saw it as a bad omen—and the sub was retired just 14 years later.

1956 – Andrea Doria Disaster
Fact: Italy's "safest ship" collided with another liner due to radar confusion. It sank, killing 46 people and ending Italy's luxury ship era.

1876 – Robbers vs. Jesse James
Fact: A gang tried robbing a bank while outlaw Jesse James happened to be inside. The robbers were outgunned and out of luck—bad timing indeed.

1976 – The $800 Billion Mistake
Fact: Ronald Wayne, Apple's third co-founder, sold his 10% stake for $800. That stake would be worth over $100 billion today. Legendary regret.

🚽 Toilet Time Trivia: Flop or Fact?

Think you remember your historical disasters? Let's test your toilet-time memory! Pick the correct answer for each epic blunder.

1. What soda company sparked national outrage by changing its classic formula in 1985?

☐ A) Pepsi   ☐ C) Coca-Cola

☐ B) RC Cola   ☐ D) Tab

2. What was the cost of NASA's Mars Climate Orbiter mission that failed due to a unit conversion error?

☐ A) $3.2 million   ☐ C) $32 million

☐ B) $327 million   ☐ D) $1 billion

3. How many times did the Soviet N1 rocket explode?

☐ A) 1   ☐ C) 3

☐ B) 2   ☐ D) 4

4. What major internet company passed on buying Google and Facebook?

☐ A) Yahoo   ☐ C) Ask Jeeves

☐ B) AOL   ☐ D) Netscape

5. How many people died when the Titanic sank?

☐ A) About 500   ☐ C) Over 1,500

☐ B) About 1,000   ☐ D) Over 2,000

Answer

1–C   2–B   3–D   4–A   5–C

5. Lost Civilizations

3300–1300 BCE – Indus Valley Civilization
Fact: The Indus Valley Civilization thrived from 3300 to 1300 BCE in what's now Pakistan and northwest India. They built planned cities with advanced drainage systems. Then, for reasons still debated—maybe climate change or dried-up rivers—they mysteriously declined.

2000 BCE–900 CE – The Maya Empire
Fact: The Maya ruled Mesoamerica for over 3,000 years, impressing the world with their math, astronomy, and writing. But drought, political unrest, and environmental damage caused their great cities to fall and be taken over by the jungle.

9500 BCE – Göbekli Tepe Mystery
Fact: Göbekli Tepe in Turkey dates back to 9500 BCE. Built by hunter-gatherers before farming began, it has huge stone pillars with carvings. Strangely, it was later buried on purpose, leaving behind a mystery that challenges how we view early civilizations.

7000–3400 BCE – Nabta Playa Stargazers

Fact: Nabta Playa in Egypt's Western Desert is the world's oldest known astronomical site. Around 7000 BCE, people built stone circles that tracked stars and seasons. But by 3400 BCE, desertification forced them to leave.

1050–1300 CE – Cahokia's Mound Builders

Fact: Cahokia was the biggest pre-Columbian city in North America, near today's St. Louis. Around 1050 CE, it had 20,000 people, massive mounds, and wooden structures to track the sun. By the 1300s, resource shortages led to its decline.

1700–1150 BCE – Sanxingdui Vanishers

Fact: The Sanxingdui civilization in China's Sichuan region existed from 1700 to 1150 BCE. They made unique bronze masks and gold items unlike anything else in China. Then they disappeared. Their amazing artifacts were only found in 1986.

100–940 CE – The Aksumite Empire

Fact: The Aksumite Empire ruled parts of Ethiopia, Eritrea, and Yemen from 100 to 940 CE. They made their own coins, created the Ge'ez script, and adopted Christianity. But climate change and new trade routes led to their fall.

802–1431 CE – Khmer Collapse

Fact: The Khmer Empire ruled Southeast Asia from 802 to 1431 CE. They built Angkor Wat and the largest pre-industrial city on Earth, with smart water systems. But climate change, invasions, and overreach caused their collapse.

5500–2750 BCE – Cucuteni-Trypillia Mystery

Fact: The Cucuteni-Trypillia culture lived in parts of Ukraine, Moldova, and Romania from 5500 to 2750 BCE. They built Europe's biggest Neolithic villages and made beautiful pottery. But they strangely burned their own towns every 60 to 80 years and eventually vanished.

2700–1420 BCE – Minoan Meltdown

Fact: The Minoans lived on Crete from 2700 to 1420 BCE. They built grand palaces with no walls for defense. But after a massive volcanic eruption and invasions from the Mycenaeans, they disappeared.

3700–1800 BCE – Norte Chico's Quiet Builders

Fact: The Norte Chico people in coastal Peru lived from 3700 to 1800 BCE. They built pyramids and farmed without using pottery or making much art. Climate change led to their decline.

1500–400 BCE – The Vanishing Olmecs

Fact: The Olmecs of southern Mexico thrived from 1500 to 400 BCE. They made giant stone heads and the first writing in the Americas. Their jaguar symbols influenced later cultures, but the Olmecs themselves vanished.

3200–1600 BCE – Dilmun's Desert Fade

Fact: The Dilmun civilization ruled Gulf trade from 3200 to 1600 BCE. They built pools, burial mounds, and used seal stamps. Mentioned in Mesopotamian legends, they disappeared when the region turned into desert.

1000 BCE–300 CE – Nok Culture's Vanishing Act

Fact: The Nok culture of Nigeria lasted from 1000 BCE to 300 CE. They were early ironworkers and made unique terracotta figures. Then they vanished, leaving no written records behind.

3300–1300 BCE – Harappa's Grid Cities

Fact: Harappa, part of the Indus Valley, built the first cities in the Indian subcontinent with grids, drains, and even bathrooms. From 3300 to 1300 BCE, they thrived—until climate and river changes led to their mysterious end.

1600–1100 BCE – Mycenaean Downfall

Fact: The Mycenaeans ruled from 1600 to 1100 BCE, building massive fortresses and inspiring Homer's tales. But when the Bronze Age collapsed, so did they—sending Greece into a 400-year dark age.

800–100 BCE – Etruscan Eclipse

Fact: The Etruscans lived in central Italy from 800 to 100 BCE, before

Rome rose. They built tombs and made luxury art. But Rome conquered them, and their language and culture faded away.

1250–1500 CE – Rapa Nui's Moai Mystery

Fact: The Rapa Nui people of Easter Island carved almost 1,000 giant moai statues between 1250 and 1500 CE. But deforestation, soil erosion, and loss of resources caused their society to collapse.

100–700 CE – Moche Vanishing

Fact: The Moche civilization in northern Peru made beautiful gold artifacts and detailed pottery from 100 to 700 CE. But they suddenly disappeared after floods and droughts caused by long-lasting El Niño events.

2700–1800 BCE – Caral Civilization Fade-Out

Fact: The Caral civilization in Peru built large pyramids and plazas between 2700 and 1800 BCE. As the oldest known urban culture in the Americas, they lived peacefully through trade. But environmental changes forced them to leave.

312 BCE–106 CE – Nabataean Stone Splendor

Fact: The Nabataeans carved stunning buildings into sandstone cliffs at Petra in modern-day Jordan from 312 BCE to 106 CE. They managed desert trade routes using advanced water systems but declined after Roman conquest and shifting trade.

500 BCE–750 CE – The Rise and Fall of the Zapotec

Fact: The Zapotec built the city of Monte Albán between 500 BCE and 750 CE in Mexico. They developed an early writing system and a major city, but warfare, drought, and unrest led to its mysterious end.

1600–1180 BCE – Hittite Empire Collapse

Fact: The Hittites ruled much of the Near East from 1600 to 1180 BCE. They were early users of iron and chariots, but their empire collapsed during the Bronze Age crisis, and their capital, Hattusa, was left in ruins.

800–1600 CE – Mississippian Mound Builders

Fact: The Mississippian culture built huge mound cities in eastern North

America from 800 to 1600 CE. Cahokia, near St. Louis, held around 20,000 people, but diseases and climate shifts caused their decline.

1500–1300 BCE – Mitanni's Disappearing Power

Fact: The Mitanni kingdom ruled parts of Mesopotamia and Syria from 1500 to 1300 BCE. They controlled trade and fought Egypt, but were later taken over by the Assyrians, leaving few direct records behind.

1070 BCE–350 CE – Kingdom of Kush's Lost Glory

Fact: The Kingdom of Kush ruled in modern Sudan from 1070 BCE to 350 CE. They once conquered Egypt and built steep pyramids, but fell after Rome changed major trade routes away from the Nile.

100–1600 CE – Ancient Puebloan Cliff Dwellers

Fact: The Ancient Puebloans, or Anasazi, lived in the American Southwest from 100 to 1600 CE. They built cliff homes and sacred kivas, but drought and conflict eventually led to their disappearance.

500–1000 CE – Wari Empire's Fall Before the Incas

Fact: The Wari Empire ruled Peru's highlands from 500 to 1000 CE. They built roads and government centers but collapsed from drought and political troubles long before the rise of the Inca.

668–935 CE – Silla Kingdom's Shaky End

Fact: The Silla Kingdom united much of Korea from 668 to 935 CE. They built temples and the world's oldest observatory but ended due to internal court problems and rebellion.

600 BCE – Lydians and the First Coins

Fact: The Lydians of western Turkey created the first standardized coins around 600 BCE. They became rich, inspiring tales like King Midas, but were defeated by the Persians in 546 BCE.

300–1000 CE – Tiwanaku's High-Altitude Innovation

Fact: The Tiwanaku people built their capital high in the Bolivian Andes from 300 to 1000 CE. They created advanced farming and stonework, but drought made the area unlivable.

11,000 BCE – Clovis and the Ice Age Exit
Fact: The Clovis culture spread across North America around 11,000 BCE. They made special spear points to hunt giant animals, but vanished when most Ice Age creatures died out.

100 BCE–500 CE – Hopewell's Sudden Stop
Fact: The Hopewell culture built huge earthworks across eastern North America from 100 BCE to 500 CE. They had wide trade routes but suddenly stopped building mounds for unknown reasons.

2300–1700 BCE – Oxus Civilization's Desert Demise
Fact: The Oxus civilization, also called the Bactria-Margiana culture, thrived in Central Asia from 2300 to 1700 BCE. They made fine metalwork and seals but disappeared due to growing deserts and climate change.

209 BCE–93 CE – Xiongnu Empire's Collapse
Fact: The Xiongnu formed the first nomadic empire on the steppe from 209 BCE to 93 CE. They threatened China so much that parts of the Great Wall were built to stop them. But internal divisions broke their unity.

1350–1530 CE – Tarascan Empire vs. the Aztecs
Fact: The Tarascan Empire ruled western Mexico from 1350 to 1530 CE. They were the Aztecs' main rivals and skilled metalworkers, but were wiped out by Spanish invasion and disease.

300 BCE–1279 CE – Chola Dynasty's Maritime Might
Fact: The Chola dynasty ruled southern India from 300 BCE to 1279 CE. They built huge temples and sent ships to Southeast Asia, but climate changes and political troubles ended their rule.

900–1470 CE – Chimú's Adobe Empire
Fact: The Chimú people built Chan Chan, the largest adobe city, in northern Peru between 900 and 1470 CE. They were conquered by the Inca, ending their civilization.

860–590 BCE – Urartu's Forgotten Kingdom
Fact: The Urartu kingdom rose around Lake Van in modern Turkey from 860 to 590 BCE. They were skilled in irrigation and metalwork but were

destroyed by the Medes and later forgotten until archaeologists found their remains.

100–940 CE – Aksumite Empire's Christian Legacy
Fact: The Kingdom of Aksum in Ethiopia made gold coins, built tall stone monuments, and became Christian in the 4th century CE. It declined by 940 CE due to climate change and trade shifts.

3200–539 BCE – Elam's Vanishing Culture
Fact: The Elam civilization of southwest Iran existed from 3200 to 539 BCE. They had their own writing and built ziggurats, but the Persians later absorbed their culture.

650–1377 CE – Srivijaya's Maritime Glory
Fact: The Srivijaya empire controlled trade in the Strait of Malacca from 650 to 1377 CE. They spread Buddhism and grew rich but fell after attacks from rival powers.

400–1100 CE – Yam Yam's Golden Trade
Fact: The Yam Yam civilization, based at Niani in modern Guinea, traded gold across Africa from 400 to 1100 CE. Drought and political breakup ended their golden age.

800–100 BCE – Etruscans Before Rome
Fact: The Etruscans ruled central Italy from 800 to 100 BCE. They built underground tombs and influenced Roman culture, but Rome later absorbed them and their language faded away.

650–1377 CE   Kerajaan Sriwijaya's Trade Power
Fact: The Kerajaan Sriwijaya empire ruled Southeast Asian trade from 650 to 1377 CE from their base in Sumatra. They got rich from shipping tolls and spread Buddhism, but lost power after attacks from rivals.

500–1000 CE – Wari's Internal Fall (Yes, Again)
Fact: The Wari Empire ruled Peru's highlands from 500 to 1000 CE. They built roads and centers but collapsed due to drought and internal divisions.

1400–1200 BCE – Tiryns and Heracles
Fact: The Tiryns civilization in Greece built strong stone forts from 1400

to 1200 BCE. It later became the legendary birthplace of Heracles but was destroyed during the Bronze Age collapse.

500 BCE–700 CE – Garamantes' Desert Farming

Fact: The Garamantes built an empire in the Libyan Sahara from 500 BCE to 700 CE. They used underground channels and fossil water to farm the desert. But over time, the water ran out and climate change forced them to abandon their cities.

1000–200 BCE – Adena's Burial Legacy

Fact: The Adena people built burial mounds across eastern North America from 1000 to 200 BCE. They processed copper from Lake Superior and traded rare materials. Their traditions later grew into what became the Hopewell culture.

900–700 BCE – Villanovan Culture's Etruscan Roots

Fact: The Villanovan culture in Italy existed from 900 to 700 BCE, before the Etruscans. They started with simple cremation burials and grew into more complex societies, eventually becoming part of Etruscan civilization.

4000–800 BCE – Dilmun's Forgotten Trade Empire

Fact: The Dilmun civilization thrived in the Persian Gulf from 4000 to 800 BCE, based in Bahrain. They acted as traders between Mesopotamia and the Indus Valley. But as power shifted in the region, their role faded.

900–200 BCE – Chavín's Highland Temples

Fact: The Chavín culture in Peru's northern highlands lasted from 900 to 200 BCE. They built stone temples and created rich religious art. But climate change and farming problems ended their influence.

802–1431 CE – Angkor's Jungle Takeover

Fact: The Angkor civilization ruled Southeast Asia from 802 to 1431 CE. They built the world's largest pre-industrial city and had advanced water systems. In the end, climate change and wars let the jungle take back their temples.

3300–1300 BCE – Harappa's Advanced Cities

Fact: The Harappan civilization built advanced cities with indoor plumbing and grid-like streets from 3300 to 1300 BCE in what is now Pakistan and northwest India. Changes in rivers and climate eventually led to their fall.

500–1000 CE – Wari's Final Collapse (One More Time)
Fact: The Wari Empire ruled much of Peru from 500 to 1000 CE. They built roads and government centers, but a long drought and growing unrest brought their rule to an end, long before the Inca rose to power.

800–200 BCE – Scythians and Steppe Warriors
Fact: The Scythians were skilled horsemen who ruled the Eurasian steppe from 800 to 200 BCE. They were known for mounted warfare and animal-style art. Over time, they were pushed out by the Sarmatians and faded from history.

2700–1420 BCE – Minoans and the Volcanic Doom (Again)
Fact: The Minoans lived on Crete from 2700 to 1420 BCE. They built large palaces without walls and created Europe's first writing system. A volcanic eruption and later invasions ended their era.

320–550 CE – Gupta's Golden Age Ends
Fact: The Gupta Empire ruled northern India from 320 to 550 CE. This was a golden age for science, art, and literature. But their power broke apart after invasions by the Huns.

500–1000 CE – Sogdians of the Silk Road
Fact: The Sogdians were merchants along the Silk Road from 500 to 1000 CE. They built trading towns in Central Asia and mixed many cultures. But Arab invasions and the rise of sea trade ended their success.

100–700 CE – Moche's El Niño Tragedy
Fact: The Moche people lived in Peru from 100 to 700 CE. They made gold art and lifelike pottery. But long El Niño events and droughts forced them to leave their desert cities.

BCE–1000 CE – The Tocharians of Tarim Basin
Fact: The Tocharians were Indo-Europeans living in China's Tarim Basin

from 2000 BCE to 1000 CE. They had their own writing and mummification. Over time, Turkic groups absorbed their culture.

3700–1800 BCE – Norte Chico's Pyramid Builders
Fact: The Norte Chico civilization in Peru lasted from 3700 to 1800 BCE. They built the first pyramids in the Americas without pottery or art. Climate shifts led to their decline.

1500–1300 BCE – Mitanni and the Assyrian Takeover
Fact: The Mitanni ruled northern Mesopotamia from 1500 to 1300 BCE. They often fought with Egypt. In the end, they were conquered by the Assyrians, and most of what we know comes from their enemies.

3200–539 BCE – Elamite Identity Lost
Fact: The Elamites lived in southwestern Iran from 3200 to 539 BCE. They had their own writing system and culture, but the Persians took over and blended them into their empire.

300–1000 CE – Tiwanaku's High-Altitude Decline
Fact: The Tiwanaku civilization built their capital high in the Andes from 300 to 1000 CE. They farmed using raised fields. A century-long drought helped bring about their collapse.

500 BCE–750 CE – Zapotec City Abandoned
Fact: The Zapotec people built Monte Albán in Mexico's Oaxaca Valley from 500 BCE to 750 CE. They developed early writing in Mesoamerica. The city was later abandoned, likely due to war and political problems.

900–1470 CE – Chimú's Mud-Brick Empire Ends
Fact: The Chimú ruled northern Peru from 900 to 1470 CE. They built Chan Chan, the largest adobe city in the Americas. The Inca conquered them and ended their rule.

100–940 CE – Aksumite Fall
Fact: The Aksumite Empire ruled parts of Ethiopia, Eritrea, and Yemen from 100 to 940 CE. They created their own script and minted coins. But climate changes and new trade routes led to their fall.

1600–1100 BCE – Mycenaean Epics and Dark Ages

Fact: The Mycenaeans ruled Greece from 1600 to 1100 BCE. They built huge stone forts and inspired Homer's epics. Their culture ended during the widespread Bronze Age collapse.

312 BCE–106 CE – Nabataean Trade Fade

Fact: The Nabataeans carved Petra into sandstone cliffs from 312 BCE to 106 CE. They managed water well and controlled trade. Rome conquered them, and trade routes shifted, ending their power.

30–375 CE – The Kushan Empire's Cultural Blend

Fact: The Kushan Empire ruled from Afghanistan to northern India from 30 to 375 CE. They blended Greek, Persian, and Indian cultures. Hun invasions eventually ended their rule.

500–1000 CE – Wari Government Falls

Fact: The Wari Empire ruled Peru's highlands from 500 to 1000 CE. They built strong centers for the government. But drought and unrest caused the system to fall apart.

1700–1150 BCE – Sanxingdui's Sudden Disappearance

Fact: The Sanxingdui civilization lived in Sichuan, China from 1700 to 1150 BCE. They made unique bronze masks and gold items unlike anything else in Chinese history. Then they vanished without clear reason.

1500–300 BCE – Phoenician Traders and Their Alphabet

Fact: The Phoenicians traded across the Mediterranean from 1500 to 300 BCE. They created the alphabet that led to Greek and Latin writing. Alexander the Great conquered them, and they were absorbed into other cultures.

2070–1600 BCE – The Mysterious Xia Dynasty

Fact: The Xia Dynasty, from 2070 to 1600 BCE, was China's first recorded dynasty. They used bronze and built irrigation systems. Overthrown by the Shang, their existence was once debated but now supported by archaeology.

1500–400 BCE – The Olmec Legacy

Fact: The Olmecs lived in southern Mexico from 1500 to 400 BCE. They made giant stone heads and the first American writing system. Their culture disappeared, but their symbols, like the jaguar, influenced later societies.

1250–1500 CE – Rapa Nui's Moai and Collapse

Fact: The Rapa Nui of Easter Island carved nearly 1,000 moai statues between 1250 and 1500 CE. But deforestation and resource loss led to their cultural collapse.

668–935 CE – Silla's Dynastic Fall

Fact: The Silla Kingdom united Korea from 668 to 935 CE. They built Buddhist temples and the world's oldest observatory. But internal problems and rebellions ended their dynasty.

331–950 CE – Caracol's Jungle Comeback

Fact: Caracol, a Maya city in Belize, ruled from 331 to 950 CE. They defeated powerful Tikal with smart alliances. Eventually, the jungle covered their vast city.

100–550 CE – Funan's Forgotten Rule

Fact: The Kingdom of Funan ruled Southeast Asia's trade from 100 to 550 CE. It was the region's first major state. It was absorbed by Chenla and is known mostly from Chinese records.

600 BCE – The First Coins by the Lydians

Fact: The Lydians in western Turkey invented the first metal coins around 600 BCE. Their wealth inspired tales like King Midas. Persia conquered them in 546 BCE.

100–1600 CE – Ancient Puebloan Cliff Dwellers

Fact: The Ancient Puebloans lived in the American Southwest from 100 to 1600 CE. They built cliff homes at places like Mesa Verde. Drought and likely conflict led to their cities being left behind.

500 BCE–700 CE – The Garamantes' Desert Empire

Fact: The Garamantes built a desert empire in the Libyan Sahara from 500

BCE to 700 CE. They used fossil water and underground irrigation, but climate change and water loss left their cities abandoned.

7000–3400 BCE – Nabta Playa's Ancient Astronomy
Fact: The Nabta Playa people lived in Egypt's Western Desert and built the world's oldest known astronomical stone site around 7000 BCE. But as the area became drier, they had to leave around 3400 BCE.

300–1000 CE – Tiwanaku's High Altitude City
Fact: The Tiwanaku civilization built their capital high in the Bolivian Andes, 12,500 feet above sea level, between 300 and 1000 CE. They created raised farms and huge stone gates, but long droughts eventually forced them to abandon their city.

1070 BCE–350 CE – Kush's Rise and Roman Fall
Fact: The Kingdom of Kush ruled over Nubia, in what is now Sudan, from 1070 BCE to 350 CE. They even conquered Egypt for a time and built tall pyramids. But when Rome shifted trade routes away from the Nile, Kush lost its power.

800–1600 CE – Mississippian Mound Builders
Fact: The Mississippian culture built huge mound cities across eastern North America from 800 to 1600 CE. Their cities had large plazas for ceremonies, but European diseases and climate change caused their way of life to collapse.

3200–539 BCE – The Elamites Fade Away
Fact: The Elamites lived in southwestern Iran from 3200 to 539 BCE. They had their own writing system and culture, but were eventually conquered by the Persians, and their identity faded away.

1000 BCE–300 CE – The Mysterious Nok
Fact: The Nok culture in northern Nigeria existed from 1000 BCE to 300 CE. They were the first in West Africa to work with iron and made unique terracotta figures. Then, without any clear reason, they disappeared.

500 BCE–1500 CE – The Dorset of Arctic Canada
Fact: The Dorset people lived in Arctic Canada from 500 BCE to 1500 CE.

They made detailed ivory carvings and tools from bone. But they vanished as the ancestors of modern Inuit, the Thule, moved into their lands.

860–590 BCE – Urartu's Forgotten Kingdom

Fact: The Urartu kingdom formed around Lake Van in today's Turkey from 860 to 590 BCE. They built canals and worked with metal, but were destroyed by the Medes. Their culture was forgotten until it was rediscovered in the 1800s.

11,000 BCE – The Clovis People's Disappearance

Fact: The Clovis people lived in North America around 11,000 BCE. They're known for their special stone spear tips. But they vanished around the same time many big Ice Age animals went extinct.

500 BCE–1600 CE – The Sao of Lake Chad

Fact: The Sao civilization lived near Lake Chad from 500 BCE to 1600 CE. They made detailed terracotta statues and bronze objects. Over time, they were absorbed into nearby kingdoms.

800 BCE–Present – The Yi People of China

Fact: The Yi people lived in China's Liangshan Mountains from 800 BCE and still exist today. They created their own writing and used bronze tools. Unlike many nearby groups, they stayed independent for thousands of years.

9500 BCE – Göbekli Tepe Mystery

Fact: Göbekli Tepe in Turkey was built around 9500 BCE. It has giant stone pillars carved with animals and was made by hunter-gatherers—before farming even began. Strangely, the builders buried it on purpose, and we still don't know why.

100 BCE–500 CE – Hopewell's Vanishing Earthworks

Fact: The Hopewell culture built huge earthworks in shapes like circles and squares across eastern North America from 100 BCE to 500 CE. They had wide trade networks, but then suddenly stopped building mounds, and no one knows why.

2500–1500 BCE – The Kerma Kingdom of Nubia

Fact: The Kerma Kingdom ruled Nubia from 2500 to 1500 BCE. They buried their dead in round tombs, sometimes with human sacrifices. Later, Egypt's New Kingdom conquered them, but their huge mud-brick structures still remain.

1600–1100 BCE – Mycenaean Collapse

Fact: The Mycenaeans ruled Greece from 1600 to 1100 BCE. They built massive stone fortresses and inspired Greek legends. Then their society collapsed, and Greece entered a 400-year dark age.

1293–1527 CE – Majapahit's Sea Empire

Fact: The Majapahit Empire ruled over parts of Indonesia and Malaysia from 1293 to 1527 CE. They built a strong sea-based trade network, but their power faded as Islamic states and the Portuguese arrived.

5500–2750 BCE – Cucuteni-Trypillia's Strange Fires

Fact: The Cucuteni-Trypillia culture lived in parts of Ukraine, Moldova, and Romania from 5500 to 2750 BCE. They built large villages and, for reasons we still don't understand, burned their homes down every 60 to 80 years.

🚽 Flush: True or Poo?

How to play: Read each statement. Choose **True** if you believe it's historically accurate or **Poo** if it sounds like baloney.

Then check below to see if your brain belongs in the history books... or the toilet! ☐

Quiz Time:

1. The pyramids of Egypt were built entirely by slaves.
☐ True   ☐ Poo

2. Vikings wore horned helmets into battle.
☐ True   ☐ Poo

3. The Mayan calendar predicted the end of the world in 2012.
☐ True   ☐ Poo

4. Every Roman dined while lying down.
☐ True   ☐ Poo

5. Cleopatra was ethnically Egyptian.
☐ True   ☐ Poo

Answer Key:

1 – Poo: Pyramids built by paid workers
2 – Poo: Horns are Hollywood, not history
3 – Poo: The calendar just reset
4 – True-ish: Only the wealthy reclined
5 – Poo: Cleopatra was Greek

6. Historical hoaxes and pranks

1957 – The Spaghetti Tree Hoax

Fact: In 1957, the BBC aired a video showing Swiss farmers picking spaghetti from trees. Many viewers believed pasta really grew on plants.

1869 – The Cardiff Giant

Fact: In 1869, George Hull buried a fake stone man in New York and charged people to see it. The hoax got so big that P.T. Barnum made a copy to cash in.

1938 – The War of the Worlds Broadcast

Fact: Orson Welles' 1938 radio show about an alien invasion scared listeners who thought it was real.

1885 – The Forgotten Art of Bed Racing

Fact: In 1885, British newspapers wrote about an "old tradition" of racing beds through the streets. It was all made up by playful reporters.

1998 – The Left-Handed Whopper

Fact: In 1998, Burger King said they made a Whopper just for left-handed people. Thousands asked for it—even though it didn't exist.

1835 – The Great Moon Hoax
Fact: In 1835, The New York Sun claimed astronomers saw bat-people living on the moon. The story helped sell lots of newspapers.

1957 – The Swiss Spaghetti Harvest
Fact: In the same 1957 prank, the BBC showed spaghetti "growing" on trees, and people called in asking how they could grow their own.

1996 – The Taco Liberty Bell
Fact: In 1996, Taco Bell said they bought the Liberty Bell and renamed it the "Taco Liberty Bell." People were upset—until they realized it was a joke.

1970s–80s – Crop Circles
Fact: In the 1970s and 80s, Doug Bower and Dave Chorley made strange patterns in English fields. People thought aliens did it, but it was just a prank.

1992 – Nixon for President
Fact: In 1992, Harvard students created a fake campaign for Richard Nixon with the slogan "He didn't do anything wrong, and he won't do it again."

1917 – The Cottingley Fairies
Fact: In 1917, two girls took photos of cardboard fairies in their garden. Even Arthur Conan Doyle believed they were real.

1770 – The Mechanical Turk
Fact: In 1770, Wolfgang von Kempelen built a fake chess-playing machine that actually had a hidden person inside controlling it.

1985 – Sidd Finch
Fact: In 1985, Sports Illustrated ran a story about a pitcher who could throw 168 mph after training with monks. It was completely fake.

2009 – The Balloon Boy
Fact: In 2009, a family said their young son floated off in a balloon. He was safe at home—it was all for publicity.

1842 – The Fiji Mermaid
Fact: In 1842, P.T. Barnum showed off a "mermaid" that was really a monkey's upper body sewn to a fish's tail.

1995 – Alien Autopsy
Fact: In 1995, Fox aired video of an alien autopsy said to be from Roswell. Later, the filmmaker admitted it was staged.

1934 – The Loch Ness Surgeon's Photo
Fact: The famous 1934 photo of Nessie turned out to be a toy submarine with a model head attached.

1923 – Lǐ Wēi's Celestial Palace
Fact: In 1923, Chinese farmer Lǐ Wēi fooled crowds by saying he built a stairway to heaven. He made money and then disappeared.

1912 – The Piltdown Man
Fact: In 1912, Charles Dawson claimed to find a fossil of a human-ape "missing link." It was fake and fooled scientists for 40 years.

1971 – The Tasaday Tribe
Fact: In 1971, a tribe in the Philippines was said to live like it was the Stone Age. Later, it was revealed they were local farmers in costumes.

1810 – Berners Street Hoax
Fact: In 1810, Theodore Hook bet he could make any house famous. He sent thousands of deliveries and visitors to one random home.

1983 – The Hitler Diaries
Fact: In 1983, Stern magazine paid millions for fake Hitler diaries. They published them before checking if they were real.

1962 – The Swedish TV Color Trick
Fact: In 1962, Swedes were told to stretch nylon stockings over their TVs to watch in color. It was just a prank.

1972 – Bearthoven Music Festival
Fact: In 1972, students at Boston University made fake brochures for a music festival featuring the made-up "Ludwig van Bearthoven."

1927 – George P. Burdell
Fact: Georgia Tech students invented a fake student in 1927. He's "graduated," "served" in wars, and "got married" over the years.

2014 – Dumb Starbucks
Fact: In 2014, comedian Nathan Fielder opened a parody coffee shop called "Dumb Starbucks," copying the real logo.

1770 – The Chess-Playing Turk (Again)
Fact: Like before, von Kempelen's 1770 machine fooled people into thinking it was a robot, but it had a hidden human inside.

1960s – The Minnesota Iceman
Fact: In the 1960s, a carnival displayed what looked like a frozen caveman. It turned out to be a latex model.

1969 – The Masked Marauders
Fact: In 1969, Rolling Stone invented a fake band with Bob Dylan and Beatles members. They even released a spoof album.

1938 – Orson Welles' War of the Worlds
Fact: The 1938 radio show made people think Martians had landed in New Jersey. It caused real panic.

1998 – The Tree Octopus
Fact: In 1998, a fake website warned about an endangered "tree octopus." Some students still believe it's real today.

1970s – Crop Circles Again
Fact: Artists Doug and Dave made field patterns in the 1970s. People thought they were made by aliens—until the duo confessed.

1903 – The Protocols of the Elders of Zion
Fact: Created around 1903, this fake document spread false claims about Jewish people. It's been completely debunked.

8th Century – The Donation of Constantine
Fact: Around the 8th century, a forged paper claimed the Roman emperor gave power to the Pope. It was fake but used for centuries.

2005 – The Los Angeles Angels of Anaheim
Fact: In 2005, the baseball team added "Anaheim" to their name, making it a confusing marketing move.

1933 – Loch Ness Monster Circus
Fact: In 1933, a circus offered a reward to catch Nessie for display—knowing it wasn't real.

1941 – Plainfield Teachers College
Fact: In 1941, a sportswriter made up a fake college and football team. They got national attention before being found out.

1817 – Princess Caraboo
Fact: In 1817, Mary Baker posed as an exotic princess from a fictional island, speaking a made-up language and fooling British high society.

1812 – The Redheffer Perpetual Motion Machine
Fact: In 1812, Charles Redheffer toured America with a "perpetual motion machine" secretly powered by a hidden crank operated by an old man eating bread.

WWII – The Van Meegeren Forgeries
Fact: Han van Meegeren sold fake Vermeer paintings to Nazis during WWII. He later proved they were forgeries to avoid treason charges for selling Dutch cultural treasures.

1736 – British Tax on Urine
Fact: Emperor Vespasian of Rome really did tax urine collection in the 1st century, but the British Parliament's alleged "Urine Collection Tax of 1736" was completely made up by satirists.

1950 – The Stone of Scone Theft
Fact: In 1950, Scottish students stole the coronation stone from Westminster Abbey and returned it months later after a nationwide search.

1814 – The Great Stock Exchange Hoax
Fact: In 1814, men in military uniforms announced Napoleon's death, causing market chaos before being revealed as fraudsters attempting market manipulation.

1976 – The Canadian Maple Syrup Strategic Reserve
Fact: Canada does maintain a real maple syrup stockpile, but the 1976 "Strategic Maple Initiative" authorizing military protection of syrup farms was completely fabricated.

1973 – Watergate Break-in Cover-up
Fact: President Nixon claimed "I am not a crook" in 1973 despite orchestrating one of history's most infamous political scandals.

1726 – The Rabbit Birth Hoax
Fact: In 1726, Mary Toft convinced doctors she was giving birth to rabbits by inserting dead bunnies into her body.

1895 – Idaho Doesn't Exist
Fact: A 1895 newspaper article jokingly claimed Idaho was a made-up name created by Congress, still cited by conspiracy theorists today.

1997 – The Dihydrogen Monoxide Ban
Fact: In 1997, a 14-year-old student gathered petitions to ban "dihydrogen monoxide" (water) based on scary-sounding but technically accurate descriptions.

1992 – Project Greek Island
Fact: The U.S. government secretly built a massive bunker beneath the Greenbrier Resort in West Virginia during the Cold War, exposed by The Washington Post in 1992.

1975 – The Yale Shower Prank
Fact: In 1975, students synchronized toilets to flush during dormitory showers, causing temperature spikes and screams heard across campus.

1992 – Pale Blue Dot Hoax
Fact: In 1992, a scientist claimed a NASA Voyager photo showed alien civilizations in distant stars, later revealed as dust on the camera lens.

Early 1900s – The Brooklyn Bridge Sale
Fact: Con artist George C. Parker repeatedly "sold" the Brooklyn Bridge to immigrants in the early 1900s, sometimes setting up toll booths until police intervened.

2008 – Bigfoot Freezer Body
Fact: In 2008, two Georgia men claimed they had a Bigfoot corpse in a freezer, which turned out to be a rubber gorilla costume.

1994 – The Microsoft Acquisition of the Catholic Church
Fact: A 1994 internet hoax claimed Microsoft was buying the Catholic Church, with the Pope becoming "Chief Spiritual Officer."

1925 – Selling the Eiffel Tower
Fact: In 1925, Victor Lustig "sold" the Eiffel Tower for scrap metal twice, convincing buyers he was a government official authorized to dismantle it.

1910 – The Dreadnought Hoax
Fact: In 1910, Horace de Vere Cole and friends (including Virginia Woolf) disguised themselves as Abyssinian royalty and were given a tour of Britain's flagship warship.

WWII – The Nazi-Proof Pigeon
Fact: During WWII, British Intelligence spread rumors that homing pigeons could detect German accents, causing Nazi soldiers to whisper around birds.

The Great Manhattan Airport Hoax
Fact: A fake historical society created elaborate plans for a never-built airport covering most of Manhattan Island, fooling architecture students for years.

1943 – The Ern Malley Affair
Fact: In 1943, two Australian poets created a fictional modernist poet whose nonsensical poems were hailed as genius before the hoax was revealed.

1920 – The Original Ponzi Scheme
Fact: In 1920, Charles Ponzi promised 50% returns in 45 days through postal reply coupons, creating the template for all future pyramid schemes.

2000 – The Bonsai Kitten
Fact: A satirical website in 2000 claimed kittens were being raised in jars to shape them like bonsai trees, triggering worldwide outrage.

1943 – Operation Mincemeat
Fact: In 1943, British intelligence dressed a corpse as an officer with fake invasion plans, allowing it to wash ashore in Spain to mislead Nazi Germany.

1998 – The Nat Tate Artwork Scam
Fact: In 1998, David Bowie and William Boyd invented an artist named Nat Tate, selling his "valuable" works to art critics who pretended to recognize his genius.

1712 – The William Lynch Speech
Fact: A purported 1712 speech on controlling slaves was widely cited academically before being exposed as a complete fabrication in the 1970s.

Ongoing – Drop Bears
Fact: Australian tour guides warn tourists about carnivorous koalas that drop from trees onto unsuspecting victims.

1996 – The Sokal Affair
Fact: In 1996, physicist Alan Sokal published nonsense disguised as postmodern philosophy in a scholarly journal to expose academic pretension.

1798 – The Illuminati Scare
Fact: A Bavarian professor's anti-Enlightenment satire in 1798 convinced many that a secret society controlled world events.

1856 – The Shakespeare Identity Question
Fact: The "Baconian theory" suggesting Francis Bacon wrote Shakespeare's works began as a parlor game in 1856 before becoming a serious conspiracy theory.

1739 – The War of Jenkins' Ear
Fact: In 1739, Britain and Spain went to war after Captain Robert Jenkins displayed his severed ear in Parliament, claiming Spanish coast guards had cut it off.

1820 – The Jefferson Bible
Fact: In 1820, Thomas Jefferson created his own Bible by cutting and

pasting only the parts he agreed with, removing all miracles and supernatural elements.

1934 – The Thunderbird Photo
Fact: A legendary photograph of cowboys holding a giant pterodactyl-like bird supposedly shot in 1890 Arizona has been "remembered" by thousands but never actually existed.

1869 – The Cardiff Giant (Again)
Fact: In 1869, tobacconist George Hull buried a fake petrified giant on his cousin's farm as an elaborate biblical hoax.

12th Century – Ancient Greek Fire Texts
Fact: Manuscripts describing the secret Byzantine weapon "Greek Fire" were fabricated in the 12th century, containing impossible chemical formulations.

Medieval – The Vegetable Lamb of Tartary
Fact: Medieval Europeans believed cotton grew from plant-sheep hybrids based on Marco Polo's misinterpreted descriptions.

1837 – The King's New Clothes
Fact: Hans Christian Andersen's 1837 tale was based on the real phenomenon of nobles pretending to see nonexistent royal garments to avoid appearing foolish.

1983 – The Hitler Diaries (Again)
Fact: In 1983, German magazine Stern paid millions for 60 volumes of fake Hitler diaries, later proven to be forgeries based on postwar paper and ink.

1972 – Nixon's Chinese Menu Prank
Fact: During his 1972 China visit, Nixon convinced journalists that a Chinese menu included "Twice-Fried Republican" and "Stewed Democratic Donkey."

1600s – The Island of California
Fact: European maps from the 1600s showed California as an island due to a novel's description being taken as geographical fact.

1909 – The President's Bathtub
Fact: William Howard Taft never actually got stuck in a White House bathtub despite being one of the most repeated "facts" about American presidents.

13th Century – The Pope Joan Legend
Fact: The medieval story of a female pope who gave birth during a procession was likely created as anti-papal propaganda in the 13th century.

1842 – The Feejee Mermaid (Again)
Fact: P.T. Barnum's 1842 attraction was actually a monkey torso sewn to a fish tail, drawing large crowds.

~490 BCE – The First Marathon
Fact: The story of Pheidippides running from Marathon to Athens to announce victory before dying was invented by Plutarch 500 years after the battle.

19th Century – Viking Horned Helmets
Fact: No archaeological evidence suggests Vikings ever wore horned helmets; the image comes from 19th-century opera costumes.

1920s – The Man Who Sold the Moon
Fact: Con artist Oscar Hartzell convinced thousands of investors in the 1920s that they could share in Sir Francis Drake's fortune once he "recovered" it.

1770 – The Chess-Playing Turk (Again)
Fact: In 1770, Wolfgang von Kempelen's automated chess-playing "machine" actually concealed a human chess master inside.

1967 – The Principality of Sealand
Fact: In 1967, Paddy Roy Bates declared an abandoned sea fort off the coast of Britain an independent nation, still "ruled" by his family today.

1934 – The Surgeon's Photo (Again)
Fact: The most famous image of the Loch Ness Monster, taken in 1934, was revealed 60 years later to be a toy submarine with a sculpted neck.

1909 – The Forgotten Pyramids of North Dakota
Fact: A 1909 newspaper article describing artificial hills in North Dakota as "American pyramids" was fabricated but still appears in some history books.

1859 – Emperor Norton I
Fact: Joshua Norton declared himself "Emperor of the United States" in 1859 San Francisco, printing his own currency that local businesses honored out of affection.

1944 – The Ghost Army
Fact: During WWII, the U.S. deployed a unit of artists and sound engineers who created inflatable tanks and fake radio transmissions to fool German intelligence.

1930 – The Day the BBC Reported No News
Fact: On April 18, 1930, the BBC evening news broadcast simply stated: "There is no news today," playing piano music instead.

Medieval – The Zanj Empire
Fact: Medieval European maps showed a vast African empire called "Zanj" based entirely on sailors' tavern tales.

1924 – Disumbrationism
Fact: In 1924, critics praised an art exhibition by fictional artist "Pavel Jerdanowitch," actually a hoax by humorist Paul Jordan-Smith to mock modern art.

1957 – The Spaghetti Harvest (Again)
Fact: The BBC aired footage in 1957 of Swiss farmers harvesting spaghetti from trees, convincing many viewers that pasta grew naturally.

1979 – Flanimals
Fact: In 1979, zoology students published a scholarly paper on nonexistent animals called "flanimals," complete with Latin names and habitat descriptions that continued to be cited for decades.

8th Century – The Donation of Constantine (Again)
Fact: A medieval forgery claimed Emperor Constantine had given the

Western Roman Empire to Pope Sylvester I in the 4th century, used to justify papal power for centuries.

1957 – The Spaghetti Tree Hoax
Fact: In 1957, the BBC aired a video showing Swiss farmers picking spaghetti from trees. Many viewers believed pasta really grew on plants.

1869 – The Cardiff Giant
Fact: In 1869, George Hull buried a fake stone man in New York and charged people to see it. The hoax got so big that P.T. Barnum made a copy to cash in.

1938 – The War of the Worlds Broadcast
Fact: Orson Welles' 1938 radio show about an alien invasion scared listeners who thought it was real.

1885 – The Forgotten Art of Bed Racing
Fact: In 1885, British newspapers wrote about an "old tradition" of racing beds through the streets. It was all made up by playful reporters.

1998 – The Left-Handed Whopper
Fact: In 1998, Burger King said they made a Whopper just for left-handed people. Thousands asked for it—even though it didn't exist.

1835 – The Great Moon Hoax
Fact: In 1835, The New York Sun claimed astronomers saw bat-people living on the moon. The story helped sell lots of newspapers.

1996 – The Taco Liberty Bell
Fact: In 1996, Taco Bell said they bought the Liberty Bell and renamed it the "Taco Liberty Bell." People were upset—until they realized it was a joke.

1970s–80s – Crop Circles
Fact: In the 1970s and 80s, Doug Bower and Dave Chorley made strange patterns in English fields. People thought aliens did it, but it was just a prank.

1992 – Nixon for President
Fact: In 1992, Harvard students created a fake campaign for Richard Nixon with the slogan "He didn't do anything wrong, and he won't do it again."

1917 – The Cottingley Fairies
Fact: In 1917, two girls took photos of cardboard fairies in their garden. Even Arthur Conan Doyle believed they were real.

1770 – The Mechanical Turk
Fact: In 1770, Wolfgang von Kempelen built a fake chess-playing machine that actually had a hidden person inside controlling it.

1985 – Sidd Finch
Fact: In 1985, Sports Illustrated ran a story about a pitcher who could throw 168 mph after training with monks. It was completely fake.

2009 – The Balloon Boy
Fact: In 2009, a family said their young son floated off in a balloon. He was safe at home—it was all for publicity.

1842 – The Fiji Mermaid
Fact: In 1842, P.T. Barnum showed off a "mermaid" that was really a monkey's upper body sewn to a fish's tail.

1995 – Alien Autopsy
Fact: In 1995, Fox aired video of an alien autopsy said to be from Roswell. Later, the filmmaker admitted it was staged.

1934 – The Loch Ness Surgeon's Photo
Fact: The famous 1934 photo of Nessie turned out to be a toy submarine with a model head attached.

1923 – Lǐ Wēi's Celestial Palace
Fact: In 1923, Chinese farmer Lǐ Wēi fooled crowds by saying he built a stairway to heaven. He made money and then disappeared.

1912 – The Piltdown Man
Fact: In 1912, Charles Dawson claimed to find a fossil of a human-ape "missing link." It was fake and fooled scientists for 40 years.

1971 – The Tasaday Tribe
Fact: In 1971, a tribe in the Philippines was said to live like it was the Stone Age. Later, it was revealed they were local farmers in costumes.

1810 – Berners Street Hoax
Fact: In 1810, Theodore Hook bet he could make any house famous. He sent thousands of deliveries and visitors to one random home.

1983 – The Hitler Diaries
Fact: In 1983, Stern magazine paid millions for fake Hitler diaries. They published them before checking if they were real.

1962 – The Swedish TV Color Trick
Fact: In 1962, Swedes were told to stretch nylon stockings over their TVs to watch in color. It was just a prank.

1972 – Bearthoven Music Festival
Fact: In 1972, students at Boston University made fake brochures for a music festival featuring the made-up "Ludwig van Bearthoven."

1927 – George P. Burdell
Fact: Georgia Tech students invented a fake student in 1927. He's "graduated," "served" in wars, and "got married" over the years.

2014 – Dumb Starbucks
Fact: In 2014, comedian Nathan Fielder opened a parody coffee shop called "Dumb Starbucks," copying the real logo.

1770 – The Chess-Playing Turk (Again)
Fact: Like before, von Kempelen's 1770 machine fooled people into thinking it was a robot, but it had a hidden human inside.

1960s – The Minnesota Iceman
Fact: In the 1960s, a carnival displayed what looked like a frozen caveman. It turned out to be a latex model.

1969 – The Masked Marauders
Fact: In 1969, Rolling Stone invented a fake band with Bob Dylan and Beatles members. They even released a spoof album.

1938 – Orson Welles' War of the Worlds
Fact: The 1938 radio show made people think Martians had landed in New Jersey. It caused real panic.

1998 – The Tree Octopus
Fact: In 1998, a fake website warned about an endangered "tree octopus." Some students still believe it's real today.

1970s – Crop Circles Again
Fact: Artists Doug and Dave made field patterns in the 1970s. People thought they were made by aliens—until the duo confessed.

1903 – The Protocols of the Elders of Zion
Fact: Created around 1903, this fake document spread false claims about Jewish people. It's been completely debunked.

8th Century – The Donation of Constantine
Fact: Around the 8th century, a forged paper claimed the Roman emperor gave power to the Pope. It was fake but used for centuries.

2005 – The Los Angeles Angels of Anaheim
Fact: In 2005, the baseball team added "Anaheim" to their name, making it a confusing marketing move.

1933 – Loch Ness Monster Circus
Fact: In 1933, a circus offered a reward to catch Nessie for display—knowing it wasn't real.

1941 – Plainfield Teachers College
Fact: In 1941, a sportswriter made up a fake college and football team. They got national attention before being found out.

1817 – Princess Caraboo
Fact: In 1817, Mary Baker posed as an exotic princess from a fictional island, speaking a made-up language and fooling British high society.

1812 – The Redheffer Perpetual Motion Machine
Fact: In 1812, Charles Redheffer toured America with a "perpetual motion

machine" secretly powered by a hidden crank operated by an old man eating bread.

1940s – The Van Meegeren Forgeries
Fact: Han van Meegeren sold fake Vermeer paintings to Nazis during WWII. He later proved they were forgeries to avoid treason charges for selling Dutch cultural treasures.

1736 – British Tax on Urine
Fact: Emperor Vespasian of Rome really did tax urine collection in the 1st century, but the British Parliament's alleged "Urine Collection Tax of 1736" was completely made up by satirists.

1950 – The Stone of Scone Theft
Fact: In 1950, Scottish students stole the coronation stone from Westminster Abbey and returned it months later after a nationwide search.

1814 – The Great Stock Exchange Hoax
Fact: In 1814, men in military uniforms announced Napoleon's death, causing market chaos before being revealed as fraudsters attempting market manipulation.

1976 – The Canadian Maple Syrup Strategic Reserve
Fact: Canada does maintain a real maple syrup stockpile, but the 1976 "Strategic Maple Initiative" authorizing military protection of syrup farms was completely fabricated.

1973 – Watergate Break-in Cover-up
Fact: President Nixon claimed "I am not a crook" in 1973 despite orchestrating one of history's most infamous political scandals.

1726 – The Rabbit Birth Hoax
Fact: In 1726, Mary Toft convinced doctors she was giving birth to rabbits by inserting dead bunnies into her body.

1895 – Idaho Doesn't Exist
Fact: A 1895 newspaper article jokingly claimed Idaho was a made-up name created by Congress, still cited by conspiracy theorists today.

1997 – The Dihydrogen Monoxide Ban
Fact: In 1997, a 14-year-old student gathered petitions to ban "dihydrogen monoxide" (water) based on scary-sounding but technically accurate descriptions.

1992 – Project Greek Island
Fact: The U.S. government secretly built a massive bunker beneath the Greenbrier Resort in West Virginia during the Cold War, exposed by The Washington Post in 1992.

1975 – The Yale Shower Prank
Fact: In 1975, students synchronized toilets to flush during dormitory showers, causing temperature spikes and screams heard across campus.

1992 – Pale Blue Dot Hoax
Fact: In 1992, a scientist claimed a NASA Voyager photo showed alien civilizations in distant stars, later revealed as dust on the camera lens.

Early 1900s – The Brooklyn Bridge Sale
Fact: Con artist George C. Parker repeatedly "sold" the Brooklyn Bridge to immigrants in the early 1900s, sometimes setting up toll booths until police intervened.

2008 – Bigfoot Freezer Body
Fact: In 2008, two Georgia men claimed they had a Bigfoot corpse in a freezer, which turned out to be a rubber gorilla costume.

1994 – The Microsoft Acquisition of the Catholic Church
Fact: A 1994 internet hoax claimed Microsoft was buying the Catholic Church, with the Pope becoming "Chief Spiritual Officer."

1925 – Selling the Eiffel Tower
Fact: In 1925, Victor Lustig "sold" the Eiffel Tower for scrap metal twice, convincing buyers he was a government official authorized to dismantle it.

1910 – The Dreadnought Hoax
Fact: In 1910, Horace de Vere Cole and friends (including Virginia Woolf) disguised themselves as Abyssinian royalty and were given a tour of Britain's flagship warship.

WWII Era – The Nazi-Proof Pigeon
Fact: During WWII, British Intelligence spread rumors that homing pigeons could detect German accents, causing Nazi soldiers to whisper around birds.

Unknown Date – The Great Manhattan Airport Hoax
Fact: A fake historical society created elaborate plans for a never-built airport covering most of Manhattan Island, fooling architecture students for years.

1943 – The Ern Malley Affair
Fact: In 1943, two Australian poets created a fictional modernist poet whose nonsensical poems were hailed as genius before the hoax was revealed.

1920 – The Original Ponzi Scheme
Fact: In 1920, Charles Ponzi promised 50% returns in 45 days through postal reply coupons, creating the template for all future pyramid schemes.

2000 – The Bonsai Kitten
Fact: A satirical website in 2000 claimed kittens were being raised in jars to shape them like bonsai trees, triggering worldwide outrage.

1943 – Operation Mincemeat
Fact: In 1943, British intelligence dressed a corpse as an officer with fake invasion plans, allowing it to wash ashore in Spain to mislead Nazi Germany.

1998 – The Nat Tate Artwork Scam
Fact: In 1998, David Bowie and William Boyd invented an artist named Nat Tate, selling his "valuable" works to art critics who pretended to recognize his genius.

1970s – The William Lynch Speech
Fact: A purported 1712 speech on controlling slaves was widely cited academically before being exposed as a complete fabrication in the 1970s.

Ongoing – Drop Bears
Fact: Australian tour guides warn tourists about carnivorous koalas that drop from trees onto unsuspecting victims.

1996 – The Sokal Affair
Fact: In 1996, physicist Alan Sokal published nonsense disguised as postmodern philosophy in a scholarly journal to expose academic pretension.

1798 – The Illuminati Scare
Fact: A Bavarian professor's anti-Enlightenment satire in 1798 convinced many that a secret society controlled world events.

1856 – The Shakespeare Identity Question
Fact: The "Baconian theory" suggesting Francis Bacon wrote Shakespeare's works began as a parlor game in 1856 before becoming a serious conspiracy theory.

1739 – The War of Jenkins' Ear
Fact: In 1739, Britain and Spain went to war after Captain Robert Jenkins displayed his severed ear in Parliament, claiming Spanish coast guards had cut it off.

1820 – The Jefferson Bible
Fact: In 1820, Thomas Jefferson created his own Bible by cutting and pasting only the parts he agreed with, removing all miracles and supernatural elements.

1934 – The Thunderbird Photo
Fact: A legendary photograph of cowboys holding a giant pterodactyl-like bird supposedly shot in 1890 Arizona has been "remembered" by thousands but never actually existed.

1869 – The Cardiff Giant
Fact: In 1869, tobacconist George Hull buried a fake petrified giant on his cousin's farm as an elaborate biblical hoax.

12th Century – Ancient Greek Fire Texts
Fact: Manuscripts describing the secret Byzantine weapon "Greek Fire"

were fabricated in the 12th century, containing impossible chemical formulations.

Medieval Period – The Vegetable Lamb of Tartary
Fact: Medieval Europeans believed cotton grew from plant-sheep hybrids based on Marco Polo's misinterpreted descriptions.

1837 – The King's New Clothes
Fact: Hans Christian Andersen's 1837 tale was based on the real phenomenon of nobles pretending to see nonexistent royal garments to avoid appearing foolish.

1983 – The Hitler Diaries
Fact: In 1983, German magazine Stern paid millions for 60 volumes of fake Hitler diaries, later proven to be forgeries based on postwar paper and ink.

1972 – Nixon's Chinese Menu Prank
Fact: During his 1972 China visit, Nixon convinced journalists that a Chinese menu included "Twice-Fried Republican" and "Stewed Democratic Donkey."

1600s – The Island of California
Fact: European maps from the 1600s showed California as an island due to a novel's description being taken as geographical fact.

Early 1900s – The President's Bathtub
Fact: William Howard Taft never actually got stuck in a White House bathtub despite being one of the most repeated "facts" about American presidents.

13th Century – The Pope Joan Legend
Fact: The medieval story of a female pope who gave birth during a procession was likely created as anti-papal propaganda in the 13th century.

1842 – The Feejee Mermaid
Fact: P.T. Barnum's 1842 attraction was actually a monkey torso sewn to a fish tail, drawing large crowds.

490 BCE (Mythical) – The First Marathon
Fact: The story of Pheidippides running from Marathon to Athens to announce victory before dying was invented by Plutarch 500 years after the battle.

19th Century – Viking Horned Helmets
Fact: No archaeological evidence suggests Vikings ever wore horned helmets; the image comes from 19th-century opera costumes.

1920s – The Man Who Sold the Moon
Fact: Con artist Oscar Hartzell convinced thousands of investors in the 1920s that they could share in Sir Francis Drake's fortune once he "recovered" it.

1770 – The Chess-Playing Turk (Again)
Fact: In 1770, Wolfgang von Kempelen's automated chess-playing "machine" actually concealed a human chess master inside.

1967 – The Principality of Sealand
Fact: In 1967, Paddy Roy Bates declared an abandoned sea fort off the coast of Britain an independent nation, still "ruled" by his family today.

1934 – The Surgeon's Photo
Fact: The most famous image of the Loch Ness Monster, taken in 1934, was revealed 60 years later to be a toy submarine with a sculpted neck.

1909 – The Forgotten Pyramids of North Dakota
Fact: A 1909 newspaper article describing artificial hills in North Dakota as "American pyramids" was fabricated but still appears in some history books.

1859 – Emperor Norton I
Fact: Joshua Norton declared himself "Emperor of the United States" in 1859 San Francisco, printing his own currency that local businesses honored out of affection.

1944 – The Ghost Army
Fact: During WWII, the U.S. deployed a unit of artists and sound engineers

who created inflatable tanks and fake radio transmissions to fool German intelligence.

1930 – The Day the BBC Reported No News
Fact: On April 18, 1930, the BBC evening news broadcast simply stated: "There is no news today," playing piano music instead.

Medieval Era – The Zanj Empire
Fact: Medieval European maps showed a vast African empire called "Zanj" based entirely on sailors' tavern tales.

1924 – Disumbrationism
Fact: In 1924, critics praised an art exhibition by fictional artist "Pavel Jerdanowitch," actually a hoax by humorist Paul Jordan-Smith to mock modern art.

1957 – The Spaghetti Harvest (Again)
Fact: The BBC aired footage in 1957 of Swiss farmers harvesting spaghetti from trees, convincing many viewers that pasta grew naturally.

1979 – Flanimals
Fact: In 1979, zoology students published a scholarly paper on nonexistent animals called "flanimals," complete with Latin names and habitat descriptions that continued to be cited for decades.

8th Century – The Donation of Constantine (Again)
Fact: A medieval forgery claimed Emperor Constantine had given the Western Roman Empire to Pope Sylvester I in the 4th century, used to justify papal power for centuries.

🚽 Fool Me Once…

Can you spot the real trick from the fake faker?
Match your wits against history's best pranksters and con artists with these five fun "Fool or Fact?" entries. Only **one** is true in each—can you flush out the fraud?

1. **Which of these actually happened?**
   A. A town in Belgium hosted an annual "Invisible Parade" with no people or floats, just marching music.
   B. A Kansas farmer convinced his town that his cow could type 60 words per minute.
   C. A German man sold the Eiffel Tower on eBay… twice.

2. **Which prankster fooled millions?**
   A) A museum in Sweden displayed an "ancient Viking game console" that turned out to be a waffle iron.
   B) The BBC once reported that Big Ben would go digital.
   C) A man sold moon rocks he claimed were harvested by retired astronauts with shovels.

3. **Which hoax was part of a war plan?**
   A) British soldiers made inflatable tanks and fake radio signals to confuse the Nazis.
   B) A fake McDonald's in Normandy was used to lure German officers into eating spoiled meat.
   C) The U.S. Navy once trained parrots to repeat enemy ship coordinates.

4. **Which one's the real hoax from history?**
   A) A fake opera singer named "Baroness Von Screech" fooled New York high society for a full season.
   B) An Australian newspaper claimed scientists found koalas naturally contain eucalyptus-flavored blood.
   C) A BBC segment once told viewers that penguins could fly—and even showed footage.

5. **Which ridiculous rumor is based in truth?**
   A) The CIA once considered using exploding cigars to assassinate Fidel Castro.
   B) Napoleon faked his own death to escape to the Bahamas.
   C) Queen Elizabeth I used invisible ink made from royal tears.

Answer:

💡 **A** – In 2009, the Belgian town of Houthalen held a parade with *nothing* in it to protest budget cuts—marching music, no marchers. Now that's silent resistance.

💡 **B** – In 1980, the BBC announced Big Ben would get a digital makeover. Outrage ensued. Fun fact: Some listeners even offered to buy the "hands" as souvenirs.

💡 **A** – The "Ghost Army" used inflatable vehicles, sound effects, and bogus broadcasts during WWII to trick the Germans. Yes, it actually worked.

💡 **C** – In 2008, the BBC aired a video of "flying penguins" for April Fool's. It looked shockingly real... until you remembered: penguins don't fly.

💡 **A** – The exploding cigar plan was *really* discussed during CIA brainstorming sessions. It never went further, but yes—it's in the files.

7. Women who changed history

1815–1852 – Ada Lovelace

Fact: Ada Lovelace wrote the first computer algorithm in 1843 for Charles Babbage's machine—before computers even existed—making her the world's first computer programmer.

1867–1934 – Marie Curie

Fact: Marie Curie discovered two elements and won two Nobel Prizes. Her notebooks are still radioactive, and people need protective gear just to handle them—her research was literally too hot to handle.

1897–1937 – Amelia Earhart

Fact: Amelia Earhart vanished while trying to fly around the world. Before that, she shattered aviation records and gender norms—her wedding announcement even stated that marriage shouldn't interfere with her work.

1914–2000 – Hedy Lamarr

Fact: Hedy Lamarr was a Hollywood star and brilliant inventor. She co-created frequency-hopping tech, which led to WiFi, GPS, and Bluetooth—all while being dubbed "the most beautiful woman in the world."

1729–1796 – Catherine the Great
Fact: Catherine the Great seized the Russian throne in a coup and ruled for 34 years. She expanded the empire and outlasted countless enemies—despite being remembered by many for one wild (and false) rumor involving a horse.

1819–1901 – Queen Victoria
Fact: Queen Victoria ruled so long they named an era after her. After her husband died, she wore black for 40 years and reportedly used cannabis for cramps—Victorian goth with a medical card.

1507–1458 BCE – Hatshepsut
Fact: Hatshepsut got tired of being regent and declared herself pharaoh. She wore a fake beard and ruled so successfully that her successor tried to erase her legacy. Archaeologists literally pieced it back together.

1820–1910 – Florence Nightingale
Fact: Florence Nightingale revolutionized nursing with data, charts, and grit. She also carried a pet owl named Athena in her pocket—because saving lives is better with bird sidekicks.

1788–1812 – Sacagawea
Fact: Sacagawea guided Lewis and Clark across the U.S. while carrying her baby. She translated with Native tribes, saved supplies from a capsized boat, and generally outperformed the whole team.

1907–1954 – Frida Kahlo
Fact: Frida Kahlo turned chronic pain into iconic art. When told she couldn't attend her own gallery opening, she showed up in an ambulance and had her bed set up in the middle of the exhibit.

1920–1958 – Rosalind Franklin
Fact: Rosalind Franklin took the X-ray photo that revealed DNA's double helix structure. Her work was used without permission, and others got the Nobel Prize—while she was mostly left out of the picture.

1412–1431 – Joan of Arc
Fact: Joan of Arc led French troops into battle as a teenager, claiming she

was guided by God. She was burned at the stake and her ashes scattered—but her legacy still burns brightly.

1822–1913 – Harriet Tubman

Fact: Harriet Tubman escaped slavery, then returned 13 times to rescue others. She carried a gun and offered no second chances for turning back. Slaveholders put a $40,000 bounty on her head.

1797–1851 – Mary Shelley

Fact: Mary Shelley wrote *Frankenstein* at just 18 during a ghost story contest with her husband and Lord Byron. She basically invented science fiction—and won the contest, naturally.

1797–1883 – Sojourner Truth

Fact: Sojourner Truth escaped slavery and became a powerful speaker despite being illiterate. Her famous "Ain't I a Woman?" speech still resonates—even though the version we quote was heavily edited by someone else.

1775–1844 – Ching Shih

Fact: Ching Shih went from sex worker to pirate queen, commanding 80,000 sailors and 1,500 ships. She banned harming women captives and later negotiated a peaceful retirement. That's a true power move.

1864–1922 – Nellie Bly

Fact: Nellie Bly faked insanity to expose abuse in an asylum. Then she raced around the world in 72 days, beating a fictional record. When told she couldn't, she packed a bag and proved otherwise.

1913–2005 – Rosa Parks

Fact: Rosa Parks didn't stay seated on that bus just because she was tired—she was a trained activist. Her quiet defiance sparked the Montgomery Bus Boycott and helped ignite the Civil Rights Movement.

1755–1793 – Marie Antoinette

Fact: Marie Antoinette never said "Let them eat cake," but she did play pretend-peasant in designer gowns. Her towering wigs were so tall, they couldn't fit through doorways—or public sympathy.

624–705 – Empress Wu Zetian

Fact: Empress Wu rose from concubine to China's only female emperor. She created a public suggestion box, crushed her enemies, and had her lovers' faces carved into cliffs. Subtle wasn't her thing.

1884–1962 – Eleanor Roosevelt

Fact: Eleanor Roosevelt redefined the role of First Lady—holding press conferences for women only and traveling so much the Secret Service nicknamed her "Rover." She pushed for human rights while making history on the move.

1906–1992 – Grace Hopper

Fact: Grace Hopper invented the first compiler and made "debugging" a thing after pulling a moth from a computer. She stayed in the Navy until age 79 and helped build the foundations of modern programming.

1821–1912 – Clara Barton

Fact: Clara Barton founded the American Red Cross after serving as a battlefield nurse during the Civil War. Even in her 90s, she delivered supplies and helped victims of disasters—fearlessly and tirelessly.

1892–1926 – Bessie Coleman

Fact: Denied flight training in the U.S. because she was Black and female, Bessie Coleman learned French, went to Europe, earned her license, and became an airshow superstar. She refused to perform for segregated audiences.

1937–present – Valentina Tereshkova

Fact: Valentina Tereshkova was the first woman in space, orbiting Earth 48 times in 1963. Before that, she worked in a textile factory and skydived for fun—so the Soviet space program figured she was qualified.

1925–2013 – Margaret Thatcher

Fact: Margaret Thatcher was the first woman to serve as Britain's Prime Minister. The Soviets called her "The Iron Lady" as an insult, but she owned it—sleeping only four hours a night and leading with force.

1697–1782 – Anne Bonny

Fact: Pirate Anne Bonny fought like a devil and revealed her gender mid-battle by flashing the enemy. Sentenced to death, she avoided execution by announcing she was pregnant. Timing was everything.

30–61 CE – Boudica

Fact: After the Romans attacked her daughters, Boudica led a brutal rebellion, burning cities and killing thousands. She lost in the end, but became such a fierce symbol that Queen Victoria claimed her as a role model.

1997–present – Malala Yousafzai

Fact: Malala was shot by the Taliban for advocating girls' education—and survived. At 17, she became the youngest Nobel Peace Prize winner, met world leaders, and still had homework that night.

1917–1984 – Indira Gandhi

Fact: Indira Gandhi was India's first and only female Prime Minister. After ordering a controversial raid on a holy site, she refused extra protection—knowing it might cost her life. It did.

1818–1894 – Amelia Bloomer

Fact: Amelia Bloomer pushed for dress reform and helped popularize "bloomers"—loose trousers under shorter skirts. Critics panicked, claiming the outfit could "unsex" women and destroy society. Spoiler: it didn't.

1939–2016 – Junko Tabei

Fact: Junko Tabei, just 4'9", became the first woman to summit Mount Everest. People told her to stay home with the kids—she chose to climb every continent's highest peak instead.

1954–present – Oprah Winfrey

Fact: Oprah grew up in poverty, sometimes wearing potato sacks as clothes. She became North America's first Black billionaire—and turned product recommendations into a cultural phenomenon known as "The Oprah Effect."

1943–present – Billie Jean King

Fact: Billie Jean King beat Bobby Riggs in the 1973 "Battle of the Sexes," with 90 million people watching. She wore rhinestone-studded tennis shoes and demolished the idea that women couldn't compete.

1939–present – Ada Yonath

Fact: Ada Yonath was mocked for trying to map ribosomes—most said it was impossible. She did it anyway and won the Nobel Prize in Chemistry. Her response to doubters? "Watch me."

1940–2011 – Wangari Maathai

Fact: Wangari Maathai started the Green Belt Movement and helped plant over 51 million trees in Kenya. When warned to stop, she replied, "I'm not afraid of anything"—and kept planting.

1858–1928 – Emmeline Pankhurst

Fact: Emmeline Pankhurst led Britain's suffragette movement with marches, hunger strikes, and smashed windows. Critics called her a rebel; she replied, "I would rather be a rebel than a slave."

1879–1966 – Margaret Sanger

Fact: Margaret Sanger opened the first birth control clinic in 1916 and was arrested for it. She watched her mother die after 18 pregnancies—and made it her life's mission to change things.

c. 370–415 CE – Hypatia of Alexandria

Fact: Hypatia was a brilliant philosopher and astronomer in ancient Egypt. She was murdered by a mob—partly for her intellect—making her possibly the first woman in history to die for science.

1838–1917 – Queen Liliʻuokalani

Fact: Queen Liliʻuokalani, Hawaii's last monarch, wrote over 160 songs and was imprisoned after a coup. She spent her time in captivity sewing a protest quilt and translating Hawaiian chants.

1908–1986 – Simone de Beauvoir

Fact: Simone de Beauvoir's book *The Second Sex* ignited modern feminism. She and philosopher Jean-Paul Sartre had such an open relationship they read each other's love letters from other partners.

1759–1797 – Mary Wollstonecraft
Fact: Mary Wollstonecraft argued for women's education in 1792 when most people thought women couldn't think logically. She had a daughter out of wedlock—who grew up to be Mary Shelley.

c. 978–1016 CE – Murasaki Shikibu
Fact: Murasaki Shikibu wrote *The Tale of Genji*, often called the world's first novel. She secretly learned Chinese by eavesdropping on her brother's lessons, since girls weren't allowed to study it.

1893–1967 – Dorothy Parker
Fact: Dorothy Parker was famous for her razor-sharp wit. When a date asked her to "say something clever," she quipped, "You've had your last chance." Mic drop, 1920s style.

1911–1989 – Lucille Ball
Fact: Lucille Ball was the first woman to run a major TV studio. She insisted on casting her Cuban husband, owned her show's episodes, and basically invented reruns—and TV royalties.

1838–1927 – Victoria Woodhull
Fact: Victoria Woodhull was the first woman to run for U.S. president—in 1872, before women could vote. She spent Election Day in jail for publishing a scandalous exposé on a preacher's affair.

1933–2020 – Ruth Bader Ginsburg
Fact: Ruth Bader Ginsburg fought for gender equality at the Supreme Court, lifted weights into her 80s, and had a workout routine so tough even her clerks could barely keep up.

1862–1931 – Ida B. Wells
Fact: Ida B. Wells was born into slavery and became a fearless journalist exposing lynchings. When her newspaper was burned down, she bought a pistol and kept writing anyway.

1942–2018 – Aretha Franklin

Fact: Aretha Franklin demanded to be paid in cash before performing, kept it in her purse, and placed it on the piano while she sang—a power move with soul.

1775–1817 – Jane Austen

Fact: Jane Austen, queen of literary romance, never married. She published anonymously and hid her writing when guests came by, pretending to sew instead.

b. 1969 – Marjane Satrapi

Fact: Marjane Satrapi created *Persepolis*, a graphic novel about growing up during Iran's Islamic Revolution. When asked why she works in the male-dominated comic world, she replied, "It's not because they have a penis that they can draw better than me."

1894–1991 – Martha Graham

Fact: Martha Graham revolutionized modern dance and kept performing into her 70s. She said, "No artist is ahead of his time. He is his time." Her moves are still tough to master today.

1768–1849 – Dolley Madison

Fact: Dolley Madison saved George Washington's portrait when the British burned the White House. She was the first to serve ice cream there and earned a lifetime seat in Congress—the only woman to do so.

1924–2005 – Shirley Chisholm

Fact: Shirley Chisholm became the first Black congresswoman in 1968 and later ran for president. She called herself "unbought and unbossed" and said being female brought more obstacles than being Black.

c. 1530–1603 – Grace O'Malley

Fact: Grace O'Malley, the Irish pirate queen, led hundreds of men and gave birth during battle—then returned to fight. She once negotiated with Queen Elizabeth I, refusing to bow because she wasn't English.

1832–1919 – Mary Edwards Walker

Fact: Mary Edwards Walker was the only woman to receive the Medal of

Honor for her work as a Civil War surgeon. She wore trousers and was once arrested for "impersonating a man." Her response: "I'm only impersonating a gentleman."

1906–1975 – Josephine Baker
Fact: Josephine Baker was a global entertainer and a WWII spy who hid messages in her sheet music. She adopted 12 children from different races and called them her "Rainbow Tribe."

1860–1926 – Annie Oakley
Fact: Annie Oakley could hit a dime tossed in the air from 90 feet away. She once shot the ash off Kaiser Wilhelm II's cigarette—and joked that missing might've prevented World War I.

1799–1847 – Mary Anning
Fact: Mary Anning found the first complete ichthyosaur fossil at age 12. She became a top fossil hunter, though male scientists often took credit for her work.

1872–1961 – Edith Wilson
Fact: Edith Wilson took over presidential duties after Woodrow Wilson's stroke in 1919. She reviewed papers, made decisions, and essentially ran the U.S. for over a year.

1821–1910 – Elizabeth Blackwell
Fact: Elizabeth Blackwell was the first woman to earn a medical degree in the U.S. The all-male class only voted to admit her as a joke—then she showed them she wasn't one.

1867–1919 – Madam C.J. Walker
Fact: Madam C.J. Walker built a haircare empire for Black women and became the first self-made female millionaire in the U.S. She drove her own car when many men couldn't afford one.

1940–1980 – Wilma Rudolph
Fact: Wilma Rudolph overcame polio and wore leg braces as a child, then won three Olympic gold medals in one year. People called her "The Black Gazelle" for her speed and grace.

1533–1603 – Queen Elizabeth I

Fact: Queen Elizabeth I ruled England for 44 years, defeated the Spanish Armada, and stayed single to keep her power. She said she had "the heart and stomach of a king."

1805–1881 – Mary Seacole

Fact: Mary Seacole was rejected by Florence Nightingale, so she funded her own trip to the Crimean War. She ran a hotel for soldiers and carried bullets in her hair—just in case.

c. 630–570 BCE – Sappho

Fact: Sappho was a Greek poet whose work celebrated women's relationships. Plato called her the "tenth Muse," and her legacy gave us the word "lesbian."

1098–1179 – Hildegard of Bingen

Fact: Hildegard of Bingen was a nun who wrote books on medicine, music, and theology. She created her own language and exchanged letters with emperors and popes—when most women weren't even allowed to read.

1744–1818 – Abigail Adams

Fact: Abigail Adams ran the family farm, gave her husband political advice, and urged him to "remember the ladies" while he helped shape the U.S. She even hung laundry in the White House.

c.1370–1330 BCE – Nefertiti

Fact: Nefertiti ruled Egypt beside her husband and may have ruled alone. Her bust, discovered in 1912, is still one of the most famous symbols of beauty in history.

1912–2004 – Julia Child

Fact: Julia Child stood 6'2", worked for the U.S. spy agency OSS during WWII, and didn't learn to cook until age 37. She once joked, "The only time to eat diet food is while you're waiting for the steak to cook."

1918–2020 – Katherine Johnson

Fact: Katherine Johnson calculated NASA's early space missions by hand.

John Glenn wouldn't fly until she double-checked the math. She worked 33 years at NASA before getting the spotlight she deserved.

1815–1902 – Elizabeth Cady Stanton
Fact: Elizabeth Cady Stanton organized the first women's rights convention in 1848. She declared, "The Bible and the Church have been the greatest stumbling blocks in the way of women's emancipation."

1593–c.1656 – Artemisia Gentileschi
Fact: Artemisia Gentileschi was a Baroque painter who overcame abuse and painted powerful women. She even joined Florence's art academy—something unheard of for women at the time.

b. 1951 – Radia Perlman
Fact: Radia Perlman created the spanning-tree protocol, which keeps the internet running. Nicknamed the "Mother of the Internet," she shrugs off the praise, saying her invention was just "mathematically obvious."

1921–2005 – Mary Jackson
Fact: Mary Jackson started at NASA as a human "computer," then became its first Black female engineer after fighting to attend segregated classes. She later helped others break barriers too.

b. 1936 – Margaret Hamilton
Fact: Margaret Hamilton led the software team for NASA's Apollo missions and coined the term "software engineering." Her code literally saved the moon landing during a critical glitch.

1875–1948 – Mileva Marić
Fact: Mileva Marić, Einstein's first wife, may have helped with his groundbreaking theories. Some historians believe her contribution to his early work was far greater than anyone admitted.

1880–1973 – Jeannette Rankin
Fact: Jeannette Rankin was the first woman elected to U.S. Congress—before women could vote nationally. She voted against both world wars, saying, "As a woman, I can't go to war, and I refuse to send anyone else."

1951–2002 – Sylvia Rivera
Fact: Sylvia Rivera fought for LGBTQ+ rights and helped lead the Stonewall uprising. She once said, "I'm not missing a minute of this, it's the revolution!"

1928–2014 – Shirley Temple
Fact: Shirley Temple was a child star during the Great Depression and later a U.S. ambassador. She helped draft the U.N.'s first human rights resolution and never let fame define her future.

1923–2014 – Stephanie Kwolek
Fact: Stephanie Kwolek invented Kevlar, the strong fiber used in bulletproof vests. She discovered it by accident and saved countless lives—with one of the greatest "oops" moments in science history.

1920–1958 – Rosalind Franklin
Fact: Rosalind Franklin took the X-ray image that revealed DNA's structure. Others used her photo without credit and won a Nobel Prize. Her vital role stayed in the shadows for decades.

1902–1992 – Barbara McClintock
Fact: Barbara McClintock discovered "jumping genes," showing that DNA can move. People ignored her for years—until she won a Nobel Prize at age 81 for being right all along.

b. 1929 – Yayoi Kusama
Fact: Yayoi Kusama turned her childhood hallucinations into art filled with polka dots and mirrors. She's lived in a psychiatric hospital by choice since 1977—and still makes art daily at 95.

1818–1900 – Elizabeth Van Lew
Fact: Elizabeth Van Lew pretended to be "Crazy Bet" so no one would suspect she was a Union spy. Her work during the Civil War helped save lives and gather crucial intelligence.

1904–1971 – Margaret Bourke-White
Fact: Margaret Bourke-White was Life magazine's first photographer and

the first female war correspondent. She photographed Nazi camps, the India-Pakistan partition, and never backed away from danger.

1868–1926 – Gertrude Bell
Fact: Gertrude Bell spoke eight languages, mapped deserts, and shaped the borders of modern Iraq. At a time when few women traveled, she was rewriting the map—literally.

1893–1952 – Hattie McDaniel
Fact: Hattie McDaniel was the first Black actor to win an Oscar, but had to sit at a segregated table during the ceremony. She broke barriers—and paid the price for doing it first.

1910–2008 – Irena Sendler
Fact: Irena Sendler smuggled 2,500 Jewish children out of the Warsaw Ghetto, hiding their names in jars buried in her yard. When captured, she never gave up a single name.

1900–1979 – Cecilia Payne-Gaposchkin
Fact: Cecilia Payne-Gaposchkin discovered that stars are mostly hydrogen. Male scientists told her to stay quiet. Decades later, the world finally realized: she had rewritten astronomy.

1909–1974 – Virginia Apgar
Fact: Virginia Apgar created the Apgar Score, used to check newborn health in the first minutes of life. She was also the first female full professor at Columbia's medical school—and played cello on the side.

b.1988 – Alexandra Elbakyan
Fact: Alexandra Elbakyan launched Sci-Hub to give free access to scientific research. Publishers sued her, but she kept going. To many, she's a modern-day Robin Hood of knowledge.

1897–1956 – Irène Joliot-Curie
Fact: Irène Joliot-Curie won the Nobel Prize with her husband for discovering artificial radioactivity. She followed in her parents' (Marie and Pierre Curie) footsteps—literally keeping Nobel Prizes in the family.

1945–1992 – Marsha P. Johnson

Fact: Marsha P. Johnson was a Black trans activist and a key figure at the Stonewall riots. When asked what the "P" stood for, she said, "Pay it no mind."

1860–1927 – Juliette Gordon Low

Fact: Juliette Gordon Low founded the Girl Scouts in 1912. Nearly deaf, she sold her pearl necklace to fund the group—and helped girls aim for the stars when society told them to stay quiet.

b.1997 – Simone Biles

Fact: Simone Biles is the most decorated gymnast in history. Her moves are so difficult they're named after her. She once said, "I'm not the next Usain Bolt or Michael Phelps. I'm the first Simone Biles."

🚽 Guess Who? – Women Who Changed History Edition

Can you identify the woman based on the clues below? No Googling while you flush!

1. I was the first woman to run for U.S. President in 1872—before women could even vote.
I spent Election Day in jail for exposing a preacher's affair.
💡 **Guess who?**

2. I helped invent Wi-Fi during WWII… while being called the "most beautiful woman in the world."
I also starred in Hollywood movies.
💡 **Guess who?**

3. I escaped slavery, then returned 13 times to help others escape.
Slaveholders offered $40,000 for my capture.
💡 **Guess who?**

4. I led French troops as a teen, said I heard voices from God, and wore armor.

After my death, people threw my ashes in the river.

💡 **Guess who?**

5. I was the first **American** woman in space—and had no pilot training. My hobby? Skydiving.

💡 **Guess who?**

Answer

1 – Victoria Woodhull
2 – Hedy Lamarr
3 – Harriet Tubman
4 – Joan of Arc
5 – Sally Ride

8. History Of Unusual Sports

1976 – Bog Snorkeling Begins
Fact: The sport of "Bog Snorkeling" was first created in Wales in 1976. Participants race through a water-filled trench cut into a peat bog, but they can't use normal swimming strokes.

2003 – Chess Boxing Invented
Fact: "Chess Boxing" was invented by Dutch artist Iepe Rubingh in 2003. It alternates between rounds of chess and boxing, with a victory coming from either a checkmate or a knockout.

Late 1800s – Wife Carrying Takes Off
Fact: "Wife Carrying" started in Finland in the late 1800s, where men race while carrying their wives through an obstacle course. The winner traditionally gets his wife's weight in beer.

15th Century – Sepak Takraw
Fact: "Sepak Takraw" has been around since the 15th century in Southeast Asia. It's like volleyball, but players can only use their feet, knees, chest, and head to touch the ball.

4000 BCE – Ancient Kabaddi

Fact: "Kabaddi" has been played in India since at least 4000 BCE. Players raid the opposing team's territory while holding their breath and chanting "kabaddi" to prove they're not inhaling.

1800s – Cheese Rolling at Cooper's Hill

Fact: The "Cooper's Hill Cheese Rolling" in England started around the 1800s. Competitors chase an 8-pound wheel of Double Gloucester cheese down a steep hill, often resulting in injuries.

10th Century – Buzkashi

Fact: "Buzkashi" has been played in Afghanistan since the 10th century. Horseback riders compete to grab a goat carcass and carry it to a scoring zone.

1997 – Extreme Ironing

Fact: "Extreme Ironing" was invented in 1997 in Leicester, England. It combines extreme outdoor activities with the satisfaction of ironing clothes.

1974 – Toe Wrestling

Fact: "Toe Wrestling" began in 1974 in Derbyshire, England. Competitors lock toes and try to pin their opponent's foot down.

1954 – Underwater Hockey

Fact: "Underwater Hockey" (also called Octopush) was invented in 1954 by British diver Alan Blake. It's played at the bottom of a swimming pool using a lead puck.

2005 – Real-Life Quidditch

Fact: "Quidditch," inspired by the Harry Potter books, became a real sport in 2005 at Middlebury College. "Broomsticks" were replaced with PVC pipes.

1970s – Ferret Legging

Fact: "Ferret Legging" started in Yorkshire, England, in the 1970s. Participants place live ferrets inside their trousers and see how long they can stand it.

17th Century – Shin Kicking

Fact: "Shin Kicking" dates back to the early 17th century in England's Cotswold Olympics. Competitors try to kick each other's shins until one person falls over.

1994 – Zorbing Invented

Fact: "Zorbing" was invented in New Zealand in 1994. It involves rolling down hills inside a large transparent plastic orb.

Ancient Tradition – Camel Wrestling

Fact: "Camel Wrestling" has been practiced in Turkey for over 2,400 years. Male camels wrestle each other during mating season to impress female camels.

1999–2010 – World Sauna Championships

Fact: The "World Sauna Championships" took place from 1999 to 2010 in Finland. The competition ended after a Russian competitor died during the 2010 finals.

2003 – Wok Racing Begins

Fact: "Wok Racing" was invented in 2003 by German TV host Stefan Raab. Competitors slide down bobsled tracks in modified Chinese woks.

2004 – Bossaball is Born

Fact: "Bossaball" was created in 2004 by Filip Eyckmans. It's a mix of volleyball, soccer, gymnastics, and capoeira played on an inflatable court with trampolines.

1980 – Joggling Championships

Fact: "Joggling" is a combination of jogging and juggling. The first world championships were held in 1980.

1980 – Man vs. Horse Marathon

Fact: The "Man vs. Horse Marathon" started in Wales in 1980 after a pub debate about whether humans could outrun horses over long distances. (Horses usually win.)

1961 – Underwater Rugby
Fact: "Underwater Rugby" was created in 1961 by German diving club members. It's played with a saltwater-filled ball at the bottom of a pool.

1990s – Moustache Championships Begin
Fact: The "Moustache Championships" have been held since the 1990s, where participants are judged on the length, style, and creativity of their facial hair.

16th Century – Hornussen in Switzerland
Fact: "Hornussen" has been played in Switzerland since the 16th century. It's like a mix of golf and baseball, where players try to hit a small puck called a "hornuss" as far as they can.

1893 – Cycle-ball Invented
Fact: "Cycle-ball" was invented in 1893 by German-American Nicholas Edward Kaufmann. Teams of two players ride bicycles and use their wheels to move a ball into goals.

15th Century – Sepak Raga Origins
Fact: "Sepak Raga" originated in 15th century Malaysia. Players stand in a circle, keeping a rattan ball in the air using any part of their body except their hands.

16th Century – Calcio Storico in Italy
Fact: "Calcio Storico" dates back to 16th century Florence, Italy. It's a brutal game combining rugby, soccer, and wrestling.

1945 – Bo-Taoshi in Japan
Fact: "Bo-Taoshi" is a Japanese capture-the-flag game created in 1945, where two teams of 150 players attack and defend a pole.

1992 – Eukonkanto World Championships
Fact: The "Eukonkanto" (Wife Carrying) World Championships have been held annually in Sonkajärvi, Finland since 1992. The winning couple gets the wife's weight in beer.

1920s – Unicycle Hockey Emerges

Fact: "Unicycle Hockey" started in the 1920s and follows similar rules to ice hockey, but it's played on unicycles with wooden sticks.

2002 – Slamball Created

Fact: "Slamball" was created in 2002 by Mason Gordon. It mixes basketball with trampolines built into the court around the basket.

2011 – Bubble Football Invented

Fact: "Bubble Football" was invented in Norway in 2011. Players are encased in inflatable bubbles that cover their upper body and head.

2003 – Chess Boxing World Championships Begin

Fact: The "Chess Boxing World Championships" have been held since 2003. Competitors alternate between rounds of chess and boxing until someone wins in one of the disciplines.

1984 – Poohsticks Goes Pro

Fact: "Poohsticks" was invented by A.A. Milne in his 1928 Winnie the Pooh books. It became a real sport with world championships held since 1984.

1267 – Gurning Contests in England

Fact: "Gurning" contests have been held in England since 1267. Competitors make the most grotesque face they can while wearing a horse collar.

1990s – Kiiking from Estonia

Fact: "Kiiking" was invented in Estonia in the 1990s. It involves swinging on a rigid swing with the goal of completing a full 360-degree rotation.

1996 – Redneck Games in Georgia

Fact: "Redneck Games" have been held in Georgia, USA since 1996. Events include mud pit belly flops and toilet seat horseshoes.

12th Century – Royal Shrovetide Football

Fact: "Royal Shrovetide Football" has been played in Ashbourne, England since the 12th century. Two teams of unlimited size try to move a ball to goals three miles apart.

1982 – Elephant Polo Begins
Fact: "Elephant Polo" was created in Nepal in 1982. It's a version of traditional polo played on elephants instead of horses.

1988 – Yukigassen Snowball Fighting
Fact: "Yukigassen" (snowball fighting) became a formal sport in Japan in 1988. Teams of seven compete in structured snowball battles.

2013 – Cheese Rolling Injuries Peak
Fact: "Cheese Rolling" at Cooper's Hill has resulted in many injuries since records began in the early 1800s. The 2013 event saw 14 people treated for injuries.

2006 – Headis: Table Tennis with Your Head
Fact: "Headis" was invented in Germany in 2006. It's a mix of table tennis and soccer, where players can only hit a special rubber ball with their heads.

2000 – Swamp Soccer World Championships
Fact: "Swamp Soccer" World Championships have been held annually in Finland since 2000. It's played on muddy bogs, making traditional soccer skills nearly useless.

1950s – Tetherball Hits Schoolyards
Fact: "Tetherball" became popular in American schoolyards in the 1950s. It's played with a ball attached to a pole by a rope, with players hitting it in opposite directions.

1970s – Disc Golf Becomes a Sport
Fact: "Disc Golf" was formalized in the 1970s, though people have been playing with flying discs since the 1920s.

1930s – Roller Derby Debuts
Fact: "Roller Derby" originated in Chicago in the 1930s during the Great Depression as an endurance competition. It evolved into its modern form in the 2000s.

1978 – Bun Climbing Festival
Fact: The "Bun Climbing Festival" has been held in Hong Kong since

1978. Competitors climb a 60-foot tower covered in steamed buns and grab as many as they can.

1998 – Apple Racing in Wisconsin

Fact: "Apple Racing" has been a tradition in Appleton, Wisconsin since 1998. Participants race hollowed-out apples with small paper sails down a rain gutter.

2006 – Egg Throwing World Championships

Fact: The "Egg Throwing World Championships" have been held in England since 2006. The current record for distance is 76.2 meters, set in 2019.

2004 – Bog Snorkeling Mountain Bike Championships

Fact: "Bog Snorkeling Mountain Bike Championships" started in Wales in 2004, combining bog snorkeling with mountain biking through water-filled trenches.

1999 – Giant Pumpkin Regatta

Fact: The "Giant Pumpkin Regatta" has been held in various locations since 1999. Competitors hollow out giant pumpkins and race them as boats.

1980 – Worm Charming Championships

Fact: "Worm Charming Championships" began in England in 1980. Competitors try to charm as many worms out of the ground as possible in 30 minutes.

🚽 Flush & Field – Sport or Satire?

You've just read about some of the strangest sports to ever grace a muddy trench, an elephant's back, or a trampoline-lined basketball court. But can you tell the **real weird sports** from the **totally made-up madness**?

Grab your toilet throne and test your sporting smarts!

Instructions: Decide whether each sport below is **REAL** or **FAKE**. (Answers at the bottom—but no peeking until you've flushed your guesses!)

#1 Extreme Office Chair Racing
Corporate competitors zoom through city streets in ergonomic battle chariots.
Sport or Satire? REAL / FAKE

#2 Snail Jousting
Contestants place tiny toothpick lances on snails and cheer as they slowly... very slowly... approach each other.
Sport or Satire? REAL / FAKE

#3 Rock-Paper-Scissors World Championship
Hundreds gather each year in Vegas to compete in high-stakes hand-symbol duels.
Sport or Satire? REAL / FAKE

#4 Underwater Paintball
A game of paintball conducted entirely beneath the surface with pressurized gel blasters and scuba masks.
Sport or Satire? REAL / FAKE

#5 Lawnmower Racing
Modified grass-cutters hit blazing speeds—because who needs grass when you have glory?
Sport or Satire? REAL / FAKE

Flush-Worthy Answer Key:

1 – **REAL!** Extreme office chair races really happen in Germany and Japan.
2 – **FAKE!** But someone should absolutely try this.
3 – **REAL!** The RPS World Championship is a legit thing. There are strategies. Serious ones.
4 – **FAKE!** Underwater paintball sounds amazing... but also like a lawsuit waiting to happen.
5 – **REAL!** Lawnmower racing exists, with people souping them up to NASCAR levels.

9. Cultural Taboos And Their Origin

2500 BCE – Touching the Pharaoh
Fact: In Ancient Egypt, around 2500 BCE, it was forbidden to touch the pharaoh because his body was seen as divine. Even accidentally brushing against him could lead to execution.

1868 – Don't Look Down on the Emperor
Fact: In Japan until 1868, commoners couldn't look down at the emperor from above. People had to close second-story windows when the emperor's procession passed by.

Early 1900s – Sacred Heads in New Zealand
Fact: In New Zealand, among the Maori, touching someone's head was taboo until the early 1900s. The head was considered sacred, and food should never be passed over it.

1837–1901 – Victorian Leg Panic
Fact: In Victorian England (1837-1901), mentioning legs in polite company was considered improper. Table legs were even covered with cloth "pantaloons" to avoid indecency.

Since the 13th Century – Don't Touch the Head in Thailand
Fact: In Thailand, since the 13th century, it's been taboo to touch someone's head, as it's believed to be the most sacred part of the body where the spirit resides.

618–907 CE – Name-Dropping Death Sentence
Fact: During China's Tang Dynasty (618-907 CE), saying the emperor's personal name was punishable by death. Historians had to use code names in official records.

Since 500 BCE – No Cheeseburgers in Orthodox Judaism
Fact: In Orthodox Jewish communities since around 500 BCE, eating milk and meat together has been prohibited, following the Torah's command not to "boil a kid in its mother's milk."

1185–1868 – Cut for Disrespect
Fact: In feudal Japan (1185-1868), samurai could kill commoners who failed to show proper respect. This was called "kirisute gomen" (permission to cut and leave).

Until the 1990s – Mourning by Amputation
Fact: Among the Dani tribe of Papua New Guinea until the 1990s, women would amputate a finger segment when a family member died, symbolizing grief and sacrifice.

Until 476 CE – No Senator Daughters for Gladiators
Fact: In Ancient Rome, until around 476 CE, actors and gladiators were celebrity figures but weren't allowed to marry senators' daughters, as entertainment was seen as dishonorable.

Early 20th Century – Foot Binding and Marriage
Fact: Until the early 20th century in China, women with unbound feet were considered unmarriageable. Foot binding started as early as age 4, causing lifelong disabilities.

500–1500 CE – Left Hand of the Devil
Fact: In Medieval Europe (500-1500 CE), left-handedness was linked to

the devil. People were forced to become right-handed, and some were even accused of witchcraft.

Until Mid-1900s – Don't Speak Their Name
Fact: Among certain Aboriginal Australian groups until the mid-1900s, saying the name of a deceased person was forbidden for years after their death, requiring creative alternatives in conversation.

16th Century – Forks Are for Fools
Fact: In 16th century England, eating with a fork was seen as unmanly, with Queen Elizabeth I being one of the few to adopt the practice while most used knives and their hands.

Until 1912 – Speak Not to the Father-in-Law
Fact: In Imperial China until 1912, women couldn't directly address their father-in-law, even if they lived in the same household, communicating through intermediaries instead.

1485–1603 – No Purple for You
Fact: In Tudor England (1485-1603), commoners couldn't wear purple, which was reserved for royalty under sumptuary laws.

650–300 BCE – State Over Baby
Fact: In ancient Sparta (650-300 BCE), not giving your newborn to the state for military training was one of the worst taboos a citizen could commit.

1920s – Devil's Violin
Fact: Until the 1920s in rural Sweden, playing the violin on Christmas Eve was believed to bring the devil to your celebration.

Around 1000 CE – Deadly Taboos
Fact: In ancient Polynesian societies (around 1000 CE), the "kapu" taboo system made certain objects, places, or actions forbidden, with violations sometimes punishable by death.

Since 7th Century – Cover That Mouth
Fact: Among the Tuareg people of the Sahara since the 7th century, men

veil their faces after puberty, with showing the mouth being seen as shamefully intimate.

1185–1600 – Untouchable Eta
Fact: In medieval Japan (1185–1600), the eta (outcasts) who dealt with dead animals were considered untouchable, forbidden from interacting with ordinary citizens.

Until 476 CE – Pants? Barbaric!
Fact: In Ancient Rome, until 476 CE, wearing pants was considered barbaric. Proper Romans wore togas despite conquering colder regions where pants were more practical.

18th Century – No Breastfeeding, That's Vulgar
Fact: In 18th century European aristocracy, upper-class women were forbidden from breastfeeding their own children. Wet nurses were hired, as breastfeeding was considered animalistic.

Until 1890s – Hush, Woman!
Fact: In 19th century America until the 1890s, women speaking in public was frowned upon. Those who did faced ridicule and social ostracism.

Since 16th Century – Mother-in-Law Gaze Avoidance
Fact: In traditional Navajo culture since the 16th century, looking directly at your mother-in-law was forbidden, requiring special avoidance behaviors when in the same area.

Around 500 BCE – The Great Bean Ban
Fact: In Ancient Greece around 500 BCE, beans were strictly taboo for followers of Pythagoras, who believed beans contained the souls of the dead or caused fetal reincarnation.

618–907 CE – Don't Laugh Openly
Fact: During the Tang Dynasty in China (618–907 CE), women were not allowed to laugh with their mouths open, as exposed teeth were seen as vulgar and sexually provocative.

16th–20th Century – Ankles? Scandalous!
Fact: From the 16th to early 20th century in Europe, showing one's ankles

was seen as inappropriate for women, with floor-length skirts required to maintain modesty.

Around 3000 BCE – Pork-Free Priests
Fact: In Ancient Egypt around 3000 BCE, priests and those entering temples were forbidden from eating pork, as pigs were associated with Set, the god of chaos.

1837–1901 – Kids Eat Separately
Fact: In Victorian England (1837–1901), it was taboo for children to eat with adults until they could demonstrate proper etiquette.

794–1185 CE – Blackened Teeth of Beauty
Fact: During Japan's Heian period (794–1185 CE), aristocratic women were expected to blacken their teeth with dye, as white teeth were considered ugly and improper.

500–1500 CE – The Talkative Woman Penalty
Fact: In Medieval Europe (500–1500 CE), it was taboo for women to speak more than their husbands in public. "Scold's bridles" were sometimes used to punish women seen as too talkative.

Until 19th Century – Eyes Down for Elders
Fact: Among certain Native American tribes until the 19th century, looking directly into the eyes of elders was considered deeply disrespectful, with eyes lowered during conversations.

Until 200 BCE – Wine Ban for Roman Women
Fact: In ancient Rome until around 200 BCE, women were prohibited from drinking wine, as it was believed that alcohol would lead to female promiscuity, and violations could be punishable by death.

1837–1901 – Pregnant? Hide Yourself
Fact: In Victorian England (1837–1901), pregnant women were expected to remain in seclusion, as pregnancy was considered too indecent to discuss in polite society.

Until 20th Century – No First Names in China
Fact: In pre-modern China until the early 20th century, calling someone

by their given name rather than their title was extremely disrespectful, except within the immediate family.

Until Early 1900s – Married Women's Silence
Fact: In traditional Korean society until the early 1900s, married women were forbidden from speaking to any man outside their immediate family, bringing shame to their household if they did.

Until 1800s – No Dining Together in Hawaii
Fact: In ancient Hawaii until the early 1800s, the kapu system prohibited men and women from eating together, with violations punishable by death.

618–907 CE – Long Nails for the Elite
Fact: During the Tang Dynasty (618–907 CE), Chinese nobles grew long fingernails on their pinky fingers to show they didn't perform manual labor. Having short nails was considered taboo for elites.

Around 500 BCE – Spartans and the Fear Taboo
Fact: In ancient Sparta around 500 BCE, showing fear in battle was the ultimate taboo. Mothers would tell their sons to "come back with your shield or on it," meaning either victorious or dead.

1500s–1800s – Coffee Crime in the Ottoman Empire
Fact: In Ottoman Turkey until the 1800s, coffee was banned several times, with coffee houses demolished and drinkers sometimes executed for being places of political dissent.

1600s–1800s – The Tomato Terror
Fact: In 17th century Europe, tomatoes were seen as poisonous and called "poison apples." They were considered dangerous because acidic tomato juice reacted with pewter plates, causing lead poisoning.

Early 1900s – Dairy Temple Ban
Fact: Among the Toda people of southern India until the early 1900s, it was forbidden for women to enter the sacred dairy temple, with violations believed to bring disaster to the community.

581–618 CE – Yellow Is for Emperors Only
Fact: During the Sui Dynasty in China (581–618 CE), wearing yellow was

forbidden unless you were the emperor, and violating this rule could lead to execution.

1837–1901 – The Trouser Taboo
Fact: In Victorian England (1837–1901), mentioning trousers in front of ladies was seen as vulgar, with terms like "inexpressibles" or "unmentionables" used instead.

100 BCE – No Purple for Roman Women
Fact: In ancient Rome around 100 BCE, women were not allowed to wear purple-bordered togas, which were reserved for male citizens. Violations resulted in legal punishment.

17th Century – Mind Your Legs in Sudan
Fact: Among the Dinka people of Sudan since at least the 17th century, stepping over someone's outstretched legs was considered offensive and believed to cause infertility.

1603–1868 – Umbrellas for the Elite
Fact: In the Edo period of Japan (1603–1868), commoners were forbidden from using umbrellas made of oiled paper, a privilege reserved for samurai and nobility.

Until 20th Century – Don't Whistle at Night
Fact: Until the early 20th century in parts of rural Ireland, whistling at night was strictly forbidden, as it was believed to summon malevolent fairies or the devil.

1800s – Dangerous Novels for Delicate Minds
Fact: In 19th century Europe, some medical professionals believed reading novels could be a mental health risk for women, thinking fiction overstimulated female brains and caused nervous disorders.

Until 600 CE – Pointing Invites Evil
Fact: In ancient China until around 600 CE, pointing with your finger was seen as rude and potentially dangerous, as it was thought to alert evil spirits to your presence.

🚽 "Taboo or Not Taboo?"

Let's play a little cultural guessing game! Below are five strange customs. Can you guess whether they were considered taboo or totally normal in their time?

1. In 18th-century France, sneezing at the dinner table was considered a sign of good health and earned you applause.

☐ A) Taboo ☐ B) Totally Normal

2. In ancient Persia, decisions made while drunk had to be confirmed sober—and vice versa.

☐ A) Taboo ☐ B) Totally Normal

3. In Medieval Iceland, calling someone a "sheep thief" could legally be answered with a duel.

☐ A) Taboo ☐ B) Totally Normal

4. In Victorian England, wearing yellow on a Tuesday was believed to bring scandal.

☐ A) Taboo ☐ B) Totally Normal

5. Among the Inuit, sharing your spouse with guests was seen as a gesture of hospitality.

☐ A) Taboo ☐ B) Totally Normal

Answers:

1: B, 2: B, 3: B, 4: A, 5: B

10. Revolutionary ideas that shocked the world

1517 – Martin Luther's Hammer Time
Fact: In 1517, Martin Luther nailed his 95 Theses to a church door in Wittenberg, challenging the Catholic Church's sale of indulgences. This act unknowingly sparked the Protestant Reformation, which would divide Western Christianity.

350 BCE – Aristotle Goes Around
Fact: Around 350 BCE, Aristotle proposed that the Earth was round, not flat. This idea shocked many people, even though earlier thinkers like Pythagoras had suggested it. Aristotle's evidence from lunar eclipses and star positions eventually convinced the educated elite.

1543 – Copernicus Spins the World
Fact: In 1543, Nicolaus Copernicus published "On the Revolutions of the Celestial Spheres" on his deathbed, suggesting the heliocentric model that the Earth revolved around the Sun. This idea contradicted 1,500 years of geocentric belief.

1859 – Darwin's Dangerous Idea

Fact: In 1859, Charles Darwin published "On the Origin of Species," presenting the theory of evolution by natural selection. He argued that humans evolved from earlier species, challenging the belief that humans were divinely created in their current form.

1905 – Einstein Bends Time

Fact: In 1905, Albert Einstein's Special Theory of Relativity proposed that time wasn't fixed but could stretch and contract depending on an observer's motion. This idea challenged long-held beliefs about the nature of reality.

1896 – Freud Gets Repressed

Fact: In 1896, Sigmund Freud suggested that unconscious sexual desires formed the foundation of human psychology. His theory shocked Victorian society, which was uncomfortable with the idea that repressed libido shaped human behavior.

1919 – Keynes Wants to Spend Big

Fact: In 1919, John Maynard Keynes published "The Economic Consequences of the Peace," arguing that governments should spend money during economic downturns. This idea went against the common belief that markets should be left to fix themselves.

4th Century BCE – Democritus Gets Tiny

Fact: In the 4th century BCE, Democritus proposed that all matter consisted of tiny, indivisible particles called atoms. This concept was so controversial that other philosophers tried to burn all his books.

1687 – Newton Drops the Apple of Truth

Fact: In 1687, Isaac Newton's "Principia Mathematica" introduced his laws of motion and universal gravitation. He showed that the universe operated like a machine, following mathematical laws instead of being controlled by divine forces.

1781 – Kant Says You Can't Trust Your Eyes

Fact: In 1781, Immanuel Kant's "Critique of Pure Reason" suggested that humans can't directly perceive reality. Instead, we experience it through mental structures, which questions our ability to truly know the world outside our minds.

1847 – Wash Your Hands, Save a Life
Fact: In 1847, Hungarian doctor Ignaz Semmelweis proposed that physicians should wash their hands between autopsies and delivering babies to reduce maternal deaths. His idea was ridiculed, as it suggested that doctors were spreading disease.

1915 – Drifting Continents? You're Joking!
Fact: In 1915, Alfred Wegener proposed the theory of continental drift, suggesting that continents moved across the Earth's surface. His idea faced strong opposition until the 1960s, when the theory of plate tectonics provided the explanation.

1633 – Galileo's Trial by Telescope
Fact: In 1633, Galileo Galilei was tried by the Inquisition for supporting Copernicus's heliocentric model. Despite his telescopic observations, he was forced to recant under the threat of torture.

1919 – Pamphlet Panic
Fact: In 1919, Mary Dennett was prosecuted for obscenity after distributing a sex education pamphlet called "The Sex Side of Life." She challenged the taboos against discussing reproduction, even for educational purposes.

1861 – Semmelweis Again, Still Ignored
Fact: In 1861, Ignaz Semmelweis published "The Etiology, Concept, and Prophylaxis of Childbed Fever," proving that handwashing could dramatically reduce maternal mortality. Yet, he was committed to an asylum, where he died after his revolutionary idea was rejected.

1748 – Morality Without Religion? Gasp!
Fact: In 1748, Baron d'Holbach shocked Europe by suggesting in "Christianity Unveiled" that morality could exist without religion. The book was publicly burned by French authorities.

1928 – Penicillin's Moldy Miracle

Fact: In 1928, Alexander Fleming discovered penicillin by accident from a contaminated petri dish. Though initially receiving little attention, it became the first antibiotic and revolutionized medicine.

1879 – Edison Lights Up the World

Fact: In 1879, Thomas Edison demonstrated the first practical incandescent light bulb after testing over 6,000 materials for the filament. This ended humanity's reliance on fire for nighttime lighting.

1846 – Doctors, Wash Again

Fact: In 1846, Ignaz Semmelweis showed that hand-washing by doctors reduced maternal mortality from 18% to 1.3%. Yet, his findings were rejected by his peers, as they implied that doctors were unintentionally killing their patients.

1936 – Turing's Thinking Machine

Fact: In 1936, Alan Turing proposed the concept of a universal computing machine, capable of performing any calculation. His idea laid the foundation for modern computers, even though most people couldn't yet understand their potential.

1993 – The Browser That Changed the World

Fact: In 1993, the Mosaic web browser introduced a graphical interface to the internet. This transformed a small academic network into the World Wide Web, even though many were skeptical that ordinary people would ever use it.

1796 – The First Shot in Vaccine History

Fact: In 1796, Edward Jenner developed the first vaccine by infecting a boy with cowpox to prevent smallpox. This was considered dangerous and ungodly at the time, as it involved introducing animal matter into humans.

1608 – A Peek Into the Cosmos

Fact: In 1608, Hans Lippershey invented the telescope, allowing people to see celestial objects that were previously invisible. This led to discoveries that eventually overturned ancient beliefs about the universe.

1440 – Move Over Monks

Fact: In 1440, Johannes Gutenberg's invention of the printing press with movable type made knowledge more accessible to the public. Despite attempts to censor printed materials, it democratized information previously controlled by elites.

1909 – Feeding the World… and the War

Fact: In 1909, Fritz Haber developed a process to synthesize ammonia from atmospheric nitrogen, enabling the production of synthetic fertilizers that would feed billions but also provide explosives for warfare.

300 BCE – Geometry Gets Serious

Fact: In 300 BCE, Euclid compiled "Elements," organizing geometry into a clear system and creating an approach to mathematics that would shape scientific thinking for centuries.

1945 – Internet Before Internet

Fact: In 1945, Vannevar Bush described the idea of a "memex" machine in "As We May Think," imagining hypertext and information retrieval systems long before the internet came to be.

1610 – Jupiter Has Friends

Fact: In 1610, Galileo published "Sidereus Nuncius," revealing his telescopic observations of Jupiter's moons, providing evidence that not all celestial bodies orbited Earth.

1953 – Cracking the Code of Life

Fact: In 1953, James Watson and Francis Crick described the double-helix structure of DNA, finally explaining how heredity works at the molecular level, a mystery that had puzzled scientists for generations.

1620 – Trust the Method

Fact: In 1620, Francis Bacon's "Novum Organum" introduced the scientific method, which emphasized systematic observation and experimentation, challenging the long-held authority of ancient texts as the ultimate source of knowledge.

1948 – Numbers That Talk
Fact: In 1948, Claude Shannon published "A Mathematical Theory of Communication," laying the foundation for information theory, which would later drive the digital revolution, even though many initially doubted its practical value.

1714 – Seeds of Change
Fact: In 1714, Jethro Tull invented the seed drill, revolutionizing agriculture and beginning the Agricultural Revolution that would transform food production and society.

1675 – Hello, Micro World
Fact: In 1675, Anton van Leeuwenhoek discovered microorganisms using his homemade microscopes, revealing a hidden world of "animalcules" that many initially dismissed as fantasy.

1662 – Chemistry vs. Alchemy
Fact: In 1662, Robert Boyle published "Skeptical Chymist," rejecting alchemy and establishing chemistry as a science based on experiments, not mystical beliefs.

1974 – The RNA Underdog
Fact: In 1974, Katalin Karikó began researching mRNA technology despite skepticism and lack of funding. Her work later played a key role in developing COVID-19 vaccines.

1869 – The Table That Predicted the Future
Fact: In 1869, Dmitri Mendeleev created the periodic table of elements, predicting the properties of yet-undiscovered elements based on patterns that many contemporaries found speculative.

1676 – The Speed of Light... Measured
Fact: In 1676, Ole Rømer measured the speed of light by observing Jupiter's moons, showing that light travels at a finite speed, challenging the belief that it was instantaneous.

1913 – Welcome to the Quantum Club
Fact: In 1913, Niels Bohr proposed that electrons orbit the nucleus in

specific energy levels, challenging classical physics and laying the groundwork for quantum mechanics.

1965 – The Echo of the Big Bang
Fact: In 1965, Arno Penzias and Robert Wilson discovered cosmic microwave background radiation, providing key evidence for the Big Bang theory, a concept that many still resisted in favor of the steady state universe model.

1633 – Descartes Hits the Brakes
Fact: In 1633, René Descartes completed "The World," proposing mechanical explanations for natural phenomena, but withheld publication after hearing about Galileo's condemnation.

1785 – Deep Time Awakens
Fact: In 1785, James Hutton presented evidence of Earth's immense age in "Theory of the Earth," challenging biblical ideas about the planet's creation with geological proof of gradual processes.

1864 – Light as Electromagnetism
Fact: In 1864, James Clerk Maxwell unified electricity and magnetism mathematically, showing that light is an electromagnetic wave and laying the groundwork for modern physics.

1886 – The First Real Car
Fact: In 1886, Karl Benz patented the first practical automobile with an internal combustion engine, changing transportation forever despite public skepticism at the time.

1895 – X-Ray Vision
Fact: In 1895, Wilhelm Röntgen discovered X-rays by accident while experimenting with cathode rays, creating the first medical imaging technology, despite early fears about "seeing through" clothing.

1964 – Quirky Little Quarks
Fact: In 1964, Murray Gell-Mann proposed quarks as the building blocks of protons and neutrons, introducing a bizarre new layer of matter that many physicists were initially reluctant to accept.

1807 – Chemistry Gets Electric
Fact: In 1807, Humphry Davy used electrolysis to isolate potassium and sodium, showing that electricity could break chemical bonds and revealing new elements.

1666 – Newton's Calculus Revelation
Fact: In 1666, Isaac Newton developed calculus to solve complex physics problems, creating a mathematical tool that could deal with continuous change when most math was focused on static quantities.

1858 – Cells Beget Cells
Fact: In 1858, Rudolf Virchow published "Cellular Pathology," proving that all cells come from other cells and that diseases stem from cellular malfunction, not from imbalances in bodily "humors."

1927 – The Universe Had a Birthday
Fact: In 1927, Georges Lemaître proposed the Big Bang theory, suggesting that the universe began from a single "primeval atom," challenging the long-held belief in an eternal, unchanging universe.

🚽 Brainstorm Blitz: Ideas That Shook the World

Ready to test your mental muscles?
Match each revolutionary thinker with their world-shaking idea. No pressure—just the fate of your trivia reputation.

Match the Genius to the Idea:
1. Albert Einstein
2. Ignaz Semmelweis
3. Mary Wollstonecraft
4. Johannes Gutenberg
5. Galileo Galilei
6. Charles Darwin
7. Katalin Karikó
8. Martin Luther

9. Alan Turing
10. Edward Jenner

Ideas:

A. Wrote 95 Theses and sparked the Protestant Reformation

B. Discovered relativity and made time bendier than a yoga instructor

C. Discovered how vaccines could prevent smallpox

D. Created the printing press and ended the monopoly on information

E. Observed Jupiter's moons and told Earth to chill—it's not the center of the universe

F. Believed women should be educated and published *A Vindication of the Rights of Woman*

G. Studied peas, pigeons, and protein messengers (and helped create mRNA vaccines)

H. Invented the concept of a universal machine—AKA the blueprint for computers

I. Said dirty hands were killing moms and suggested a radical new idea: soap

J. Proposed evolution by natural selection and scared every Victorian with a Bible

Answer Key:

1 → B, 2 → I, 3 → F, 4 → D, 5 → E, 6 → J, 7 → G, 8 → A, 9 → H, 10 → C

11. Architecture that defied logic

1173 – The Leaning Tower of Pisa
Fact: The Leaning Tower of Pisa started leaning during its construction in 1173, all because it was built on a shallow three-meter foundation set in weak soil. Still, engineers pressed on and added seven more stories to the already tilted base.

1886–1922 – Winchester Mystery House
Fact: The Winchester Mystery House in California was under constant construction from 1886 to 1922. Built by Sarah Winchester, the house features staircases that lead to ceilings, doors that open into walls, and 160 rooms that connect in a seemingly random maze.

Early 12th Century – Angkor Wat's Stone-by-Stone Construction
Fact: Angkor Wat in Cambodia, built in the early 12th century, involved moving 5 million tons of sandstone from a quarry 25 miles away—basically, the same as relocating the Great Pyramid of Giza, one stone at a time.

2004 – The Crooked House in Poland
Fact: The Crooked House in Sopot, Poland, built in 2004, was designed with warped walls and melting facades, making it look like something out of a dream—or a hallucination.

1882–Present – Gaudí's Still-Unfinished Sagrada Família
Fact: Antoni Gaudí's Sagrada Família in Barcelona has been under construction since 1882 and is still unfinished. Its complex shapes and bone-like columns are so intricate that they needed computer modeling just to make sense of them.

800 CE – Chand Baori's Mind-Bending Geometry
Fact: Chand Baori in India, built around 800 CE, is a symmetrical wonder with 3,500 steps arranged in a precise geometric pattern, plunging 13 stories into the earth—an astonishing feat for ancient builders.

1984–1997 – The Heaviest Building on Earth
Fact: The Palace of Parliament in Bucharest, Romania, built between 1984 and 1997, is the heaviest building on Earth. Made of 700,000 tons of steel and bronze, a million cubic meters of marble, and 900,000 cubic meters of wood, it's so massive that it reportedly sinks 6mm every year.

1416 – Ice Road Engineering in Beijing
Fact: To build Beijing's Forbidden City, massive marble blocks weighing up to 330 tons were moved using a 30-mile-long ice path in 1416. Workers sprayed water along the route from wells every 500 meters to keep the surface slippery.

1919 – The World's Smallest Skyscraper
Fact: The Newby-McMahon Building in Texas, built in 1919, earned the nickname "world's smallest skyscraper" after investors missed that the blueprints were drawn in inches instead of feet. The result? A building only 40 feet tall and 10 feet wide.

2005–Present – Bolivia's Bold "Cholets"
Fact: Bolivia's eye-catching "Cholets," designed by architect Freddy

Mamani since 2005, defy architectural norms with their bold colors and gravity-challenging designs inspired by Aymara traditions.

Early 1900s–2014 – The Mystery of the Moving Rocks

Fact: In Death Valley's Racetrack Playa, large rocks mysteriously move across the desert floor, leaving visible tracks. The mystery, observed since the early 1900s, was finally solved in 2014—thin sheets of ice pushed by the wind were behind it.

1996 – The Dancing House in Prague

Fact: The Dancing House in Prague, completed in 1996, looks like it's being pinched in the middle. With its curved "Fred and Ginger" design, the structure challenges traditional ideas of balance and form.

64 CE – Nero's Rotating Dining Room

Fact: Emperor Nero's rotating dining room in his Domus Aurea palace, built around 64 CE, reportedly turned continuously during meals while guests were showered with perfume and flower petals—a marvel of ancient engineering that still puzzles historians.

1967 – Habitat 67's Floating Cubes

Fact: Montreal's Habitat 67, completed in 1967, is made up of 354 identical concrete cubes stacked in a way that seems random. Many hang over empty space, held up by little visible support, giving it a surreal, gravity-defying look.

2007 – The Upside Down House in Poland

Fact: The Upside Down House in Szymbark, Poland, completed in 2007, is exactly what it sounds like—built with its roof in the ground and foundation pointing up. A specially engineered steel frame inside keeps the whole thing standing.

1990 – The Hang Nga "Crazy" Guesthouse

Fact: The Hang Nga Guesthouse in Vietnam, built in 1990, looks like it melted into existence. With animal-shaped rooms and tree-like structures, its surreal design seems structurally impossible—yet it's held up for decades.

1990s – The McMansion Mashups
Fact: America's McMansions of the 1990s often mashed together clashing styles—Palladian windows, Tudor beams, and Greek columns all in one house—earning them a reputation as disasters of architectural logic.

2005 – The Twisting Turning Torso
Fact: The Turning Torso in Malmö, Sweden, completed in 2005, twists 90 degrees from bottom to top over 54 floors. Its unusual shape demanded an innovative support system to keep it from collapsing under the stress.

1862 – Boston's Skinny Spite House
Fact: Boston's "Skinny House," built in 1862, is just 10.4 feet wide at its widest point. Legend says it was built out of spite—to block a brother's view after a feud over a Civil War inheritance.

1987–Ongoing – The Ryugyong Hotel's Pyramid Problem
Fact: The Ryugyong Hotel in Pyongyang began construction in 1987, but for 16 years it stood unfinished. Its pyramid shape was so ambitious that engineers simply couldn't figure out how to complete it.

1250 CE – Easter Island's Wandering Giants
Fact: Easter Island's stone statues, carved from 1250 CE onward, weigh up to 86 tons each. Somehow, they were moved as far as 11 miles—using methods that archaeologists are still trying to explain.

1995 – The Wooden Gangster Skyscraper
Fact: In Archangelsk, Russia, the Wooden Gagster House was built in 1995 by gangster Nikolai Sutyagin. It grew to 13 stories tall—144 feet—without any formal plans, until authorities tore it down for being a safety hazard.

1939 – Fallingwater's Falling Worries
Fact: Frank Lloyd Wright's Fallingwater, completed in 1939, stretches boldly over a waterfall. Engineers warned the concrete cantilevers would eventually fail—and in 2002, the structure needed steel reinforcement to save it.

1345 – The Ponte Vecchio's Riverside Real Estate
Fact: Florence's Ponte Vecchio, finished in 1345, holds three stories of shops right on top of a bridge. Some structures even dangle over the river's edge, centuries before building codes existed.

1999 – The Sail-Shaped Skyscraper
Fact: The Burj Al Arab in Dubai, completed in 1999, was built on an artificial island with an outer fabric that mimics a sail—designed to hold up against harsh desert windstorms despite not being load-bearing.

1684 – Versailles' Giant Mirror Factory
Fact: The Hall of Mirrors at Versailles, built in 1684, required oversized glass panels that didn't yet exist. A glass factory was created solely to produce the 357 mirrors that line its walls today.

2010 – Antilla: Asymmetry as Architecture
Fact: Mumbai's Antilla residence, completed in 2010, has 27 stories—and not one of them is identical. Sections are deliberately built at odd angles, breaking every rule of symmetry in design.

7th Century BCE–Ongoing – The Impossible Wall
Fact: The Great Wall of China, built over centuries starting in the 7th century BCE, crosses wildly different terrains. In some places, it clings to 45-degree mountain slopes, defying gravity and time.

2012 – The Shard's Open-Topped Peak
Fact: The Shard in London, completed in 2012, has an open-top design where the glass panels don't meet at the very peak. It looks unfinished on purpose—open to the elements by design.

1958 – The Giant Iron Atom in Brussels
Fact: Brussels' Atomium, built in 1958, looks like a giant iron crystal blown up 165 billion times. Its spherical "atoms" are linked by tubes with escalators inside, ignoring all typical floor plans.

126 CE – The Pantheon's Unreinforced Miracle
Fact: The Pantheon in Rome, completed around 126 CE, features a huge unreinforced concrete dome with a circular opening at the top. According

to modern engineering, it shouldn't stand—but it has for nearly 2,000 years.

2003 – The Blinding Beauty of Disney Hall
Fact: Frank Gehry's Walt Disney Concert Hall in Los Angeles, completed in 2003, originally reflected so much sunlight off its curved metal surfaces that it overheated sidewalks and temporarily blinded passing drivers.

1989 – The Bubble House's Curve Obsession
Fact: The "Bubble House" near Cannes, designed in 1989 by Antti Lovag, is a dreamy maze of interconnected, bubble-like rooms. It avoids straight lines and right angles entirely—challenging everything we think we know about building design.

1902 – The Flatiron Wager
Fact: The Flatiron Building in New York, completed in 1902, was so thin and tall that people once placed bets on how far debris would fly when the wind knocked it down. Over a century later, it's still standing strong.

1973 – Sydney's Impossible Opera
Fact: The Sydney Opera House, finished in 1973, took 16 years to build. The original design by Jørn Utzon won a competition in 1957—but it was so complex, engineers had to rethink how to build it from scratch.

1992–2008 – The Wooden Tower That Shouldn't Be
Fact: Russia's Sutyagin House, started in 1992 and demolished in 2008, climbed to 13 stories and 144 feet—made entirely of wood. It was built without plans or training, just lumber and raw intuition.

1649 – The Palace in the Clouds
Fact: The Potala Palace in Tibet, completed in 1649, stands over 12,000 feet above sea level. Built without modern machinery, its stone walls are 16 feet thick at the base and hold more than 1,000 rooms in thin air.

1883 – Elephants on the Bridge
Fact: When the Brooklyn Bridge opened in 1883, it was the world's first steel-wire suspension bridge—and people feared it would collapse. To prove its strength, the engineer sent 21 elephants across it.

1990 – The Tower That Offended Feng Shui
Fact: The Bank of China Tower in Hong Kong, finished in 1990, has a jagged geometric design that breaks all symmetry—and even offends feng shui so deeply that nearby buildings added mirrors to deflect the bad luck.

2011 – The Skateable Home
Fact: In Malibu, the "skateboard house" designed by Pierre Andre Senizergues in 2011 is more than just skate-friendly—it's entirely skateable. Walls, ceilings, every inch is rideable.

2004 – A Skyscraper with a Swinging Heart
Fact: Taipei 101 in Taiwan, completed in 2004, was built directly on a fault line and in a typhoon zone. To stay upright, it relies on a massive 728-ton steel pendulum—visible to the public—that balances the entire tower.

1561 – Domes So Good They Blinded the Builder
Fact: Moscow's St. Basil's Cathedral, completed in 1561, doesn't look like anything else in Russian architecture. Its onion domes and asymmetry were so unique that legend says Ivan the Terrible blinded the architects to stop them from ever repeating it.

2002 – Library of Light and Glass
Fact: The Bibliotheca Alexandrina in Egypt, finished in 2002, has the world's largest uninterrupted glass roof. Its design mimics a giant sundial, partially buried in the earth, casting light onto the books below.

2018 – Skyscrapers in Stone Forests
Fact: In China's Guizhou province, the Stone Forest Skyscrapers, completed in 2018, rise from jagged karst formations long thought unbuildable. Engineers had to anchor the towers deep into the limestone caves below.

2013 – Seoul's Scaled Super Towers
Fact: The Dancing Dragons towers in Seoul, finished in 2013, shimmer with movement. Their facades are covered in scale-like panels that open and close automatically, breathing life into the skyline.

1994–Present – The World's Tallest Slum

Fact: The Torre de David in Caracas was left half-built in 1994—but squatters moved in, turning it into the tallest slum in the world. With no elevators or finished walls, over 3,000 people carved out a vertical community of their own.

3600 BCE – Malta's Mysterious Megastructures

Fact: Malta's Stone Age temples, built around 3600 BCE, still baffle archaeologists. With no metal tools, builders moved 50-ton stones, carved out perfect acoustics, and aligned structures to the stars.

🚽 "Would You Build It?" Quiz

Let's play architect for a minute. Below are a few real and totally fake architectural ideas. Can you sniff out the true marvels from the blueprint baloney?

Circle **"YES"** if you think it's real, or **"NO"** if you think someone built it in their imagination... maybe while stuck in traffic (or on the toilet).

#1 A hotel shaped like a giant dog, complete with a head you can sleep in.
Would You Build It? **YES / NO**

#2 A museum entirely underground, with exhibits that rotate—literally—on a moving track.
Would You Build It? **YES / NO**

#3 A skyscraper in Dubai designed to fold open during the day like a flower.
Would You Build It? **YES / NO**

#4 A chapel made entirely from ice and fish bones, rebuilt every winter in Norway.
Would You Build It? **YES / NO**

#5 A bridge in Vietnam shaped like a golden dragon that breathes fire at night.
Would You Build It? **YES / NO**

Time to Unveil the Blueprints! (Answers)

1 – **YES** – It's real! The **Dog Bark Park Inn** in Idaho welcomes you to sleep inside a beagle-shaped B&B.
2 – **NO** – Sounds cool, but engineers would rather not deal with rotating walls.
3 – **NO** – Dubai loves wild ideas, but this one is just petal-pushing fantasy.
4 – **NO** – Ice chapels are real... fish bone ones, not so much.
5 – **YES** – The **Dragon Bridge** in Da Nang, Vietnam actually breathes fire on weekends!

12. Historical Events That Were Almost Forgotten

1919 – The Great Molasses Flood
Fact: In 1919, a storage tank in Boston burst, unleashing 2.3 million gallons of molasses that surged through the streets at 35 mph. The sticky wave killed 21 people in what became known as the Great Molasses Flood.

1904 – The Cheating Marathon Champion
Fact: At the 1904 Olympic marathon in St. Louis, runner Fred Lorz hitched a car ride for 11 miles, then jogged across the finish line to claim victory—until officials realized the truth and disqualified him.

1859 – The Solar Storm That Almost Hit
Fact: Back in 1859, Earth narrowly escaped a catastrophe when a powerful solar storm just missed us. If it had hit, it would've wiped out global telegraph systems and sparked devastating fires.

1908 – Art Medals at the Olympics
Fact: The 1908 London Olympics weren't just about sports—they also

handed out medals for art. Architecture, sculpture, painting, literature, and music were all part of the Games until 1948.

1974 – 10-Cent Beer Night Mayhem
Fact: In 1974, the Cleveland Indians hosted a "10-Cent Beer Night." Unlimited cheap booze led to a riot, fans streaking across the field, and players dodging hot dogs and firecrackers.

1942 – The Battle of Los Angeles
Fact: During World War II, in 1942, U.S. troops fired over 1,400 anti-aircraft shells into the night sky over Los Angeles—targeting what turned out to be harmless weather balloons.

1967 – The Disappearing Prime Minister
Fact: In 1967, Australian Prime Minister Harold Holt went for a swim at Cheviot Beach and vanished without a trace. He was never found.

Roman Era – The Vanishing Town of Silchester
Fact: The ancient Roman town of Silchester remains a mystery. It was abandoned so slowly and carefully that archaeologists are still baffled by why its residents ever left.

1788 – The Battle of Karánsebes (with themselves)
Fact: In 1788, Austrian troops, confused and panicked, mistakenly opened fire on each other in the Battle of Karánsebes. Over 10,000 soldiers died—all on the same side.

1848 – London's Staggering Contest
Fact: London once held a Staggering Contest in 1848, where participants got extremely drunk and tried to walk in a straight line. The prize? Cold hard cash.

1972 – The Cod Wars
Fact: In 1972, Iceland and the United Kingdom clashed in the "Cod Wars" over fishing rights. Ships collided, nets were cut—but not a single person died in the salty standoff.

1518 – The Dancing Plague
Fact: In 1518, a bizarre event gripped Strasbourg: hundreds of people

started dancing uncontrollably in the streets. Some danced for days—until they literally dropped dead.

1923 – The Dead Jockey Who Won
Fact: Jockey Frank Hayes won a race at Belmont Park in 1923—even though he died mid-race from a heart attack. His body stayed balanced on the horse all the way to victory.

1932 – The Great Emu War
Fact: In 1932, Australia went to war—with emus. The giant birds were destroying crops, so soldiers brought in machine guns. The emus won.

1961 – Nuclear Near-Miss in North Carolina
Fact: In 1961, the U.S. Air Force accidentally dropped two hydrogen bombs on North Carolina. Miraculously, neither detonated—avoiding what could've been a massive disaster.

1855 – Toronto's Circus Riot
Fact: The 1855 Toronto Circus Riot started when a group of clowns got into a fight with firefighters. Chaos spread across the city, sparked by a few angry performers.

1976 – The Train Baby and Hero Driver
Fact: In 1976, a Tokyo train driver braked so hard to avoid missing a stop that a pregnant woman went into labor. He delivered the baby—and still got everyone to their stations on time.

1874 – The Drunken Derby
Fact: During the 1874 Kentucky Derby, nearly every jockey was drunk. The result? One of the messiest races in the sport's history.

1886 – The Lobster Salad Panic
Fact: In 1886, New York was gripped by the Lobster Salad Panic. A false rumor claimed tainted lobster had killed party guests, sparking citywide hysteria—though no one actually died.

1859 – Emperor Norton Rises
Fact: In 1859, San Francisco newspapers mistakenly reported that Joshua Norton had declared himself "Emperor of the United States." Rather than

correct the hoax, they leaned into it—publishing his proclamations for decades.

1851 – Handle Heist at the Great Exhibition
Fact: At the 1851 Great Exhibition in London, organizers had to redesign the public toilets. Visitors, unfamiliar with flush mechanisms, kept stealing the handles as souvenirs.

1967 – Sweden's Drive-Side Switch
Fact: In 1967, Sweden switched from driving on the left to the right in a single day. The event, known as "Dagen H," was expected to cause chaos—but only 157 minor accidents were reported.

1979 – The Antarctic Book Spoiler Stabbing
Fact: In 1979, tensions in Antarctica reached a breaking point when a Soviet scientist stabbed a colleague for constantly spoiling the endings of the books he was reading.

1814 – The London Beer Flood
Fact: Back in 1814, a massive vat at a London brewery burst, sending 320,000 gallons of beer flooding the streets. The tragic Beer Flood killed eight people.

1930 – The Pi Bill
Fact: In 1930, the Indiana legislature nearly passed a bill legally defining the value of pi as 3.2. It took a math professor to step in and stop the madness.

67 CE – Nero Wins by Falling Off
Fact: Emperor Nero competed in the Olympic chariot race in 67 CE, fell off his chariot, didn't finish—yet was still declared the winner.

1956 – The Plane, the Bar, and the Drunk Dare
Fact: In 1956, Tommy Fitzpatrick, drunk and on a dare, stole a small plane and landed it flawlessly on a Manhattan street in front of a bar. Two years later, he did it again.

1940s – Project X-Ray and the Bat Bombs
Fact: During WWII, the U.S. developed "Project X-Ray," a plan to drop

bats carrying tiny incendiary bombs over Japan. The idea was eventually scrapped.

1962 – The Laughter Epidemic
Fact: In 1962, thousands in Tanganyika (now Tanzania) were struck by a strange condition, uncontrollable laughter. It lasted nearly a year and even forced schools to shut down.

1325 – Possessed Statue Prank
Fact: In 1325, a wooden statue of the Virgin Mary spun wildly during a church service in Belgium. Mass panic followed—until someone discovered a boy was hiding inside and causing chaos.

1940s – Japan Accidentally Bombs an Outhouse
Fact: During WWII, Japan bombed Oregon. The only damage? A single church toilet—accidentally blown up by local police while trying to dispose of the bomb.

1631 – Thou Shalt Commit Adultery?
Fact: In 1631, a printing error in a Bible left out the word "not" in the commandment "Thou shalt not commit adultery." The result was the infamous "Wicked Bible."

1925 – The War of the Stray Dog
Fact: The War of the Stray Dog in 1925 kicked off when a Greek soldier chased his dog across the border into Bulgaria and was shot, sparking an international crisis.

1904 – Strychnine and Gold Medals
Fact: At the 1904 Olympics, marathon runner Thomas Hicks was given strychnine—yes, rat poison—and brandy by his trainers to keep him going. He won gold, but nearly died doing it.

1874 – Attack of the Locust Swarm
Fact: In 1874, a colossal swarm of locusts swept across the American Midwest. It stretched 110 miles wide and 1,800 miles long, with an estimated 12.5 trillion insects consuming everything in sight.

1816 – The Year Without a Summer

Fact: The year 1816 became known as the "Year Without a Summer" after Mount Tambora's eruption triggered global cooling. Crops failed, snow fell in Italy—and Mary Shelley wrote Frankenstein.

1998 – Honoring the Elusive POW

Fact: In 1998, a Japanese town built a statue honoring an American POW pilot they never managed to capture during WWII—impressed by his remarkable ability to evade them.

1951 – The Cable-Cutting Repairman

Fact: In 1951, a repairman named Elwin was suspended beneath a bridge when he accidentally cut the only supporting cable. He rode the entire structure down—and survived with just minor injuries.

1992 – How to Win the Lottery on Purpose

Fact: In 1992, an Australian gambling syndicate bought almost every ticket in the Virginia lottery. They hit the $27 million jackpot and still made a profit after covering their massive costs.

1828 – Jackson's Cannibal Campaign

Fact: During the 1828 election, Andrew Jackson's opponents accused him of cannibalism—claiming he had eaten Native American corpses. He still won the presidency.

🚽 Forgotten But Fantastic: Mini Memory Quiz!

1. Which Olympic athlete won a race while technically dead?

- ☐ A) Thomas Hicks
- ☐ C) Frank Hayes
- ☐ B) Fred Lorz
- ☐ D) Nero

2. Which food item was not responsible for mass panic or disaster?

- ☐ A) Beer
- ☐ C) Molasses
- ☐ B) Lobster Salad
- ☐ D) Popcorn

3. Who lost a fight to a flightless bird?

☐ A) Andrew Jackson ☐ C) The Australian Army

☐ B) The Emus ☐ D) The Ostriches

4. Which event involved a crowd so intoxicated, the players had to run for cover?

☐ A) The Kentucky Derby of 1874

☐ B) 10-Cent Beer Night

☐ C) The Lobster Salad Panic

☐ D) The Staggering Contest

5. Which ruler was declared an Olympic winner after falling off his chariot?

☐ A) Julius Caesar ☐ C) Napoleon

☐ B) Emperor Nero ☐ D) Harold Holt

Answer Key:

1 – C, 2 – D, 3 – C, 4 – B, 5 – B

13. The Oddest Items Used as Currency

Ancient Rome – The Original Paycheck

Fact: Salt was so valuable in ancient Rome that soldiers were sometimes paid with it. That's where we get the word "salary," from the Latin salarium.

Medieval Russia – Fur for Funds

Fact: In medieval Russia, squirrel pelts were considered legal currency. Tax collectors even had to collect "one marten skin from each house."

Modern Italy   The Cheesiest Bank Vaults

Fact: In Italy, Parmesan cheese has been used as loan collateral. Some banks have entire vaults dedicated to storing thousands of cheese wheels.

Ancient China – Stone Tools, Tiny Price

Fact: In parts of ancient China, people used tiny jade carvings of everyday items, like tools, as currency. They were miniature stone versions of the real things.

Mongolia & Tibet – Brick by Brick
Fact: Tea bricks once served as currency in Mongolia, Siberia, and Tibet. They came in different grades and could even be eaten in emergencies.

WWII – Smokes for Survival
Fact: In WWII prison camps, cigarettes became the go-to currency. The trading system was so consistent that economists later studied it as a model of natural currency development.

Yap Island – Heavy Money
Fact: On the Island of Yap, giant stone discs called Rai stones are still considered money. Some are so massive, they're never moved—just verbally transferred.

California Gold Rush – Moo-lah
Fact: John Sutter, who kicked off the California Gold Rush, didn't use gold at his fort. Instead, he minted his own tin coins called "Sutters," stamped with a star and simple images of farm animals.

Australia, 1800s – Rummy Economy
Fact: Until the 1800s, rum was a common form of currency in Australia. When officials tried to crack down on it, it led to the Rum Rebellion of 1808.

Solomon Islands – Smile Worth a Tooth
Fact: In parts of the Solomon Islands, dolphin teeth are still used as currency. Their value depends on the size and color of each tooth.

Ancient India – Shelling Out
Fact: Ancient India relied on cowrie shells as currency. They were so dependable that some regions officially used them well into the 1800s.

U.S. Prisons, 2004 – Mackerel Market
Fact: After a smoking ban hit U.S. federal prisons in 2004, mackerel packets replaced cigarettes as currency. One pack was roughly worth a dollar.

Germany, 1923 – Stamp of Approval
Fact: During Germany's 1923 hyperinflation, postage stamps stuck to

cardboard became more useful than paper money—and people used them as cash.

Soviet Georgia, 1970s – Potato Paychecks
Fact: In 1970s Soviet Georgia, potatoes temporarily replaced cash. Workers were literally paid in spuds when money ran short.

Colonial America – Beads of Value
Fact: Native Americans used wampum—beads made from shells—as currency. European colonists later adopted it when they ran low on coins.

Ancient China – Knife Money
Fact: Ancient China also had "knife money"—bronze knives with holes in the handles so they could be strung together and carried like coins.

Medieval England – Splitting the Bill
Fact: Medieval England used wooden sticks called tally sticks as currency. Notches showed the amount owed, and the stick was split lengthwise so each party kept a half.

Borneo – Heads or Tails?
Fact: Some headhunting tribes in Borneo used human skulls as currency up until the early 20th century.

Modern Italy – Cheese Bank, Part 2
Fact: Parmigiano Reggiano cheese is still accepted as collateral by certain Italian banks, which keep it safe in climate-controlled cheese vaults.

Maya Civilization – Bittersweet Money
Fact: The ancient Maya used cacao beans as currency. Some counterfeiters even hollowed them out and filled them with mud to fake their value.

11th-Century Bohemia – Hair Money
Fact: In 11th-century Bohemia, tiny silver coins known as "hair money" were minted to be woven directly into the monarch's hair.

19th-Century Texas – The Guano Economy
Fact: In the 19th century, bat guano—yes, bat droppings—was so valuable

in parts of Texas and New Mexico that people used it to make purchases and settle debts.

Nauru, Until 1940s – Vomit Value
Fact: On the island of Nauru, large polished slabs of petrified whale vomit, also known as ambergris, were used as currency until the 1940s.

Zimbabwe, 2008 – Tasty Tender
Fact: During Zimbabwe's 2008 hyperinflation crisis, one company printed money on edible rice paper—so if the cash lost its value, at least people could eat it.

Central Africa – Copper X-Currency
Fact: In central Africa, Katanga crosses—X-shaped copper ingots—were used as money. Their value often depended on the sound they made when struck.

American Frontier – Wire Worth
Fact: Sections of barbed wire were traded as currency on the American frontier. The more effective the barb style was at deterring cattle, the more valuable it was.

1990s Russia – Vodka Paychecks
Fact: After the economic collapse in 1990s Russia, vodka became a de facto currency. Many workers were actually paid in bottles.

Ancient Mesopotamia – Debt Tablets
Fact: In ancient Mesopotamia, people used clay tablets that recorded debt obligations. These tablets often changed hands to settle new debts—essentially functioning as currency.

Silk Road – Sippable Savings
Fact: Bricks of dried tea leaves were used as currency along the Silk Road. In times of scarcity, merchants sometimes ate their own money.

Fiji – Whale of a Currency
Fact: In Fiji, whale teeth were once used as money. The larger and more well-formed the tooth, the greater its worth.

World War I, France – Playing Card Cash
Fact: During World War I, some French towns ran so low on metal that they printed emergency currency on playing cards.

Ancient Southeast Asia – Broken China Bucks
Fact: In ancient Southeast Asia, porcelain fragments became so valuable that people would intentionally break fine china just to create more currency units.

Hawaii – Feather Fund
Fact: In Hawaii, colorful kingbird feathers were used as currency. Feathery hats made from them essentially acted as the kingdom's treasury reserve.

Papua New Guinea – Skull Coinage
Fact: In Papua New Guinea, people used kapkap—decorated skull pieces made from turtle shell and giant clam shell—as currency.

Ancient Greece – Obeloi Economics
Fact: Before coins became common, ancient Greeks sometimes used iron cooking skewers, known as obeloi, as money.

Native American Tribes – Pointed Payments
Fact: Among some Native American tribes, arrowheads were traded as currency. The better the craftsmanship, the higher their value.

Ethiopia Until 1930s – Salty Salary
Fact: In Ethiopia, salt bars were used as currency until the 1930s. Merchants would even lick them to check for quality.

West Africa – Beaded Banking
Fact: Coral beads were so prized in West Africa that they remained in use as currency well into the 20th century.

South Pacific – Boar Banknotes
Fact: In parts of the South Pacific, boar tusks curled into full circles served as currency. Their value depended on the size and perfection of the curl.

Asian Trade Routes – Tea with a Seal
Fact: Compressed blocks of fermented tea leaves, known as "tea money,"

were used along Asian trade routes. To prevent counterfeiting, officials stamped the blocks with special seals.

🚽 Toilet Timeline Trivia:
Flush-Worthy Firsts Edition

Think you're the king or queen of quirky knowledge? Test your wits on these "firsts" that deserve a seat on the porcelain throne of history.

1. What was the first food eaten on the Moon?
   Answer:

2. Who made the first ever phone call—and what did he say?
   Answer:

3. What's the first recorded item sold on eBay?
   Answer:

4. Who was the first person to go over Niagara Falls in a barrel... and survive?
   Answer:

5. What's the world's first documented recipe for?
   Answer:

ANSWER:

1 – Bacon cubes and coffee

2 – Alexander Graham Bell: "Mr. Watson, come here, I want to see you."

3 – A broken laser pointer

4 – Annie Edson Taylor

5 – Beer (Sumerian recipe, 1800 BCE)

14. Unexpected Alliances in History

1936 – Nazi Scientists Join Team America
Fact: After World War II, the U.S. launched Operation Paperclip—recruiting Nazi scientists to help with space and missile programs, including some who had once built weapons to bomb Allied cities.

1939 – Frenemies with a Pact
Fact: The 1939 Molotov-Ribbentrop Pact between Nazi Germany and the Soviet Union left the world stunned, as the two nations had long denounced each other's ideologies.

13th Century – Knights and Mongols?
Fact: Back in the 13th century, European Christians even considered aligning with the Mongol Empire to try and defeat Muslim powers in the Middle East.

1770s – France's Unexpected Crush on American Rebels
Fact: During the American Revolution, Catholic France supported the Protestant American rebels in their fight against Protestant Britain—setting aside religion for politics.

1960s – Communist BFF Breakup
Fact: Though communist allies in the 1950s, China and the Soviet Union nearly went to nuclear war in the 1960s over ideological clashes and border disputes.

1940s – Finland's Neutral-but-Not Alliance
Fact: During World War II, Finland was in a strange spot. It was allied with Nazi Germany but kept friendly ties with Britain—and refused to persecute its Jewish citizens.

1500s – When France Dined with the Ottomans
Fact: Back in the 1500s, the Muslim Ottoman Empire and Christian France teamed up, mainly to go against their shared rival, Habsburg Austria.

1972 – Nixon's Red Carpet Moment
Fact: In 1972, President Richard Nixon—known for being strongly anti-communist—surprised the world by opening diplomatic relations with communist China, going against years of U.S. policy.

1812 – Sweden's Napoleon Fan Club
Fact: In 1812, Sweden made a surprising choice by picking one of Napoleon's marshals, Jean-Baptiste Bernadotte, to be their crown prince—even though Sweden was at war with France at the time.

1836 – Viva la Revolución, Mexi-Texan Style
Fact: During the Texas Revolution, some Mexican citizens actually fought side by side with the Texians to oppose Santa Anna's centralist rule.

1895 – Tea and Kimonos with the British
Fact: In 1895, Britain and Japan formed an alliance—despite Britain's usual habit of avoiding formal alliances and Japan's recent step out of isolation.

1914 – East Africa Meets the East Asian Powerhouse
Fact: In 1914, Christian Ethiopia and Shinto Japan formed a unique alliance. Ethiopia saw Japan as a successful example of modernizing without being colonized by Western powers.

1720 – Direct Dial to the Crown
Fact: In 1720, the Iroquois Confederacy took a bold step—they sent their own ambassadors straight to the British Crown, skipping over colonial governments, to form a direct alliance.

1860s – Confederacy's European Dream Team
Fact: During the American Civil War, the Confederate States tried to build ties with Britain and France—even though both of those countries had already banned slavery.

1940s – Axis Pen Pals with Secrets
Fact: Though Nazi Germany and Imperial Japan were allies in World War II, they rarely worked closely together and often kept major operations secret from each other.

1980s – Double-Crossing Diplomacy
Fact: During the Iran-Iraq War in the 1980s, the U.S. secretly supported both sides at different times—and sometimes even at the same time.

1936 – The King and the Führer
Fact: In 1936, Britain's King Edward VIII formed a friendship with Adolf Hitler, raising serious concerns about his role as monarch and contributing to his decision to step down.

1914 – Japan's Opportunistic Leap
Fact: While European countries fought each other in World War I, Japan used its alliance with Britain as a reason to grab German colonies in China and the Pacific.

1569 – Poland and Lithuania, BFFs
Fact: In 1569, Poland and Lithuania united their two countries—even after years of conflict—and created one of Europe's largest and longest-lasting states.

1940s – Communists and Commandos
Fact: During World War II, British special forces fought alongside communist fighters in Yugoslavia, putting aside their political differences to fight a common enemy.

1920 – A Split in Support
Fact: In the 1920 Polish-Soviet War, France supported Poland by sending military advisors, while Britain offered moral support—putting the former allies on different sides.

1918 – Everyone vs. the Bolsheviks
Fact: After the Russian Revolution, anti-communist "White" Russian forces teamed up with countries like Britain, France, Japan, and the U.S. to fight the new Bolshevik government.

1914 – Weaponizing Religion
Fact: In 1914, Germany encouraged the Ottoman Empire to declare a religious war—hoping that Muslims living under British, French, and Russian control would rise up against them.

1960s – Mossad's Moroccan Collaboration
Fact: In the 1960s, Israeli intelligence (Mossad) worked with Moroccan agents to target and reportedly assassinate Moroccan opposition leader Mehdi Ben Barka.

1979 – Red-on-Red Conflict
Fact: In 1979, communist China invaded communist Vietnam—proving that national interests often mattered more than shared ideology.

1980s – From Friend to Foe
Fact: In the 1980s, President Ronald Reagan gave military aid to Saddam Hussein's Iraq during its war with Iran—only for the U.S. to go to war against Iraq a few years later.

1941 – A Strange Bedfellows Invasion
Fact: In 1941, Britain and the Soviet Union—despite not getting along politically—worked together to invade Iran to secure vital supply routes during World War II.

Post-WWII – From Axis to Ally
Fact: After World War II, the U.S. welcomed fascist Spain as an ally against communism, even though Spain had earlier supported the Axis powers.

1950s – Nasser Plays Both Sides

Fact: In the 1950s, Egypt's President Nasser cleverly balanced both sides of the Cold War—getting economic aid from the U.S. while buying military gear from the Soviet Union.

1960s – Albania Picks a New Friend

Fact: For a short time in the 1960s, communist Albania sided with China against the Soviet Union—creating one of the strangest alliances of the Cold War.

1962 – A Banana Republic's Cold War Shuffle

Fact: Honduras briefly considered switching recognition from Taiwan to Communist China in 1962—until the U.S. offered economic aid to keep the alliance intact.

1985 – Israel Sells Weapons to Iran

Fact: During the Iran-Contra Affair, Israel secretly funneled U.S. weapons to Iran—even while Iran was labeled part of the "Axis of Evil."

1801 – U.S. and Sweden vs. Pirates

Fact: In the early 1800s, the United States and Sweden joined forces to fight Barbary pirates in North Africa, marking one of America's earliest military alliances.

1980s – CIA and Afghan Mujahideen

Fact: During the Soviet-Afghan War, the CIA backed Afghan mujahideen fighters—some of whom would later become part of the Taliban.

1917   Greek Royal Drama Meets World War

Fact: In 1917, Britain and France forced the pro-German King Constantine of Greece to abdicate so Greece could join the Allies.

1943 – Churchill and Stalin's Friendly Toasts

Fact: Winston Churchill and Joseph Stalin once got so drunk together at the Tehran Conference that translators had to bow out—and Churchill allegedly climbed onto a chair to make a toast.

1791 – U.S. and Native Tribes Team Up

Fact: In an unusual 18th-century alliance, some Native American tribes helped U.S. troops fight rival tribes during the Northwest Indian War.

1945 – France and Ho Chi Minh's Brief Cooperation

Fact: After WWII, Ho Chi Minh tried to negotiate Vietnamese independence by cooperating with France—only for both sides to clash shortly after.

2001 – NATO Invokes Article 5

Fact: After the 9/11 attacks, NATO invoked Article 5 for the first time ever—an attack on one was considered an attack on all—uniting members in support of the U.S.

1940s – OSS and the Mafia Team Up

Fact: America's wartime spy agency (the OSS) partnered with the Mafia to gather intelligence and sabotage Axis operations in Sicily.

🚽 Toilet Time Top 3s

Top 3 Most Awkward Diplomatic Gifts:

A pair of donkeys – Gifted by a Middle Eastern ruler to Queen Victoria. She was... unimpressed.

A taxidermied alligator in a suit – Sent to a U.S. governor in the 1920s. It still haunts an office somewhere.

2 tons of cheese – Napoleon once sent this to a king. The royal court nearly revolted—over the smell.

Top 3 Most Ironic Historical Injuries:

Confucius – Said to value peace and harmony… and may have died from a beating.

President Zachary Taylor – Died after eating too many cherries and drinking cold milk at a July 4th picnic.

Tycho Brahe – The great astronomer died because he didn't want to leave a royal banquet to pee.

👑 Top 3 Strangest Royal Hobbies:

King George III – Loved farming so much, people called him "Farmer George."

Emperor Nero – Thought he was a great actor and made senators attend his plays. Or else.

Queen Christina of Sweden – Collected mummies and had a secret room of skulls. Totally normal, right?

😈 Top 3 Most Petty Historical Revenge Moves:

Peter the Great – Forced nobles to shave their beards, then taxed the ones who didn't.

Napoleon – Named a cannon after a critic, then used it in a demonstration.

Cardinal Richelieu – Outlawed dueling just so he could eliminate annoying nobles.

😬 Top 3 Unexpected "Oops" Moments in History:

The Great Chicago Fire – Possibly started by a cow knocking over a lantern.

The Leaning Tower of Pisa – Leaned from day one... and they just kept building.

The Eiffel Tower – Hated by Parisians when first built. Now it's their pride and postcard.

15. Weirdest Jobs People Have Done in History

Rome, 1st–5th centuries CE – Urine Collectors

Fact: In ancient Rome, urine collectors gathered human urine from public toilets to sell to tanners and launderers, who valued its ammonia for cleaning fabrics and softening leather.

Egypt, 3000 BCE–30 BCE – Professional Mourners

Fact: Professional mourners were hired in ancient Egypt to cry loudly and dramatically at funerals, often paid based on the intensity of their wailing and visible sorrow.

England, 1760s–1920s – Knocker-Uppers

Fact: Knocker-uppers made a living in Victorian England by waking people up for work. They'd tap on bedroom windows with long sticks or shoot dried peas through blowpipes to get the job done.

England, 1400s–1800s – Gong Farmers

Fact: Medieval gong farmers had the unenviable task of collecting human waste from cesspits and privies. They worked only at night since doing so during the day was illegal due to the odor and mess.

England, 1530s–1700s – Whipping Boys
Fact: Whipping boys were raised alongside young princes and punished in their place since royalty couldn't be struck. The idea was that seeing a friend suffer would correct the prince's behavior.

Wales/England/Scotland, 1600s–1900s – Sin-Eaters
Fact: Sin-eaters were paid to attend funerals, eat food passed over the deceased, and symbolically absorb their sins—saving the soul of the dead while burdening their own.

England/Netherlands, 1500s–1800s – Dog Whippers
Fact: Dog whippers worked in churches to keep stray dogs from disturbing services, using small whips or tongs to gently escort the animals out.

Europe, 1600s–1900s – Professional Rat Catchers
Fact: Professional rat catchers were common across Europe and sometimes wore clothing decorated with dead rats as a grim advertisement for their services.

China/Japan, Tang Dynasty–1900s – Ear Cleaners
Fact: Ear cleaners practiced their craft in public spaces like teahouses, using intricate tools to gently remove earwax while offering a soothing and oddly satisfying service.

England/America, 1850s–1920s – Restorers of Lost Manhood
Fact: Restorers of lost manhood were Victorian-era con men who promised to cure impotence with questionable devices like electric belts and radioactive underwear.

Rome, 1st century BCE–5th century CE – Orgy Planners
Fact: Ancient Rome even had designated orgy planners, whose job was to organize everything from the guest list to food and entertainment for elite parties.

Britain/Ireland, 1740s–1920s – Human Alarm Clocks
Fact: Human alarm clocks once walked morning routes, tapping on

people's windows with long poles to wake them up before alarm clocks were widely used. Rain or shine, they were the reliable wake-up call of the working class.

Rome, 1st century BCE–5th century CE – Armpit Hair Pluckers
Fact: In ancient Roman bathhouses, professional armpit hair pluckers used bronze tweezers to remove underarm hair for clients who took grooming very seriously—even back then.

Europe, 1700s–1800s – Leech Collectors
Fact: Leech collectors earned their living by wading into swamps and ponds with bare legs, waiting for leeches to latch on. Once full of blood, they'd pluck them off and sell them for medical treatments.

Scotland, 1500s–1600s – Golf Ball Divers
Fact: Golf ball divers retrieved balls from murky water hazards, risking injury—or worse—since the expensive, feather-stuffed golf balls couldn't be easily replaced.

England, 1800s–1900s – Pure Finders
Fact: Pure finders roamed Victorian London's streets collecting dog poop, which they then sold to tanneries for use in the leather-making process. Yes, people literally made a living selling dog feces.

United States/Europe, 1950s–1970s – Keypunch Girls
Fact: Keypunch girls were the early computer world's unsung heroes, manually entering programming data into punch cards—often faster than the machines could even keep up.

Europe/Middle East, 1st–17th centuries – Fullers
Fact: Fullers worked by stomping on freshly woven cloth soaked in human urine. It helped clean and thicken the fabric.

Britain/America, 1700s–1830s – Body Snatchers
Fact: Body snatchers secretly dug up fresh graves to sell corpses to medical schools for anatomy lessons, before laws allowed legal cadaver donations. Grave-robbing was literally a business.

Europe, 1300s–1700s – Plague Doctors
Fact: Plague doctors treated patients during deadly outbreaks, dressed in eerie bird-like masks filled with herbs. Despite their creepy look, most had little to no medical training.

🚽 Bathroom Trivia — True or False?

Ready to separate fact from flush-worthy fiction?
1. A man once sued himself and won.
2. Ancient Egyptians shaved off their eyebrows to mourn the death of their cats.
3. Viking helmets always had horns.
4. The shortest war in history lasted only 38 minutes.

Answers:

1 – **True** (He sued himself while in prison—and technically won, though he didn't get any money.)
2 – **True** (Those cats were sacred, and eyebrows were optional.)
3 – **False** (No horns—thank you, Hollywood.)
4 – **True** (The Anglo-Zanzibar War of 1896. Blink and you missed it.)

🚽 Bathroom Trivia— True or False?

Let's test your truth detector!
1. In medieval times, animals could be put on trial.
2. Bananas grow on trees.
3. The Eiffel Tower can grow taller in the summer.
4. Albert Einstein failed math as a student.

Answers:

1 – **True** (Pigs, rats, even insects were summoned to court—tiny lawyers not included.)
2 – **False** (They grow on massive herbs, not trees. Banana drama!)
3 – **True** (It can grow up to 6 inches taller due to heat expansion.)
4 – **False** (He actually aced math—blame the myth, not the man.)

16. Strange Historical Coincidences

Robert Todd Lincoln – A Presidential Curse Magnet
Fact: Abraham Lincoln's son, Robert Todd Lincoln, had an eerie connection to presidential tragedies. He was present—or nearby—when three U.S. presidents were assassinated: his own father, James Garfield, and William McKinley.

1910 – Mark Twain's Comet Farewell
Fact: Mark Twain once predicted he'd go out with Halley's Comet, the same way he came in. And he did—born in 1835 when the comet was visible, and dying in 1910 when it returned.

1898 – The Titan and the Titanic
Fact: In 1898, writer Morgan Robertson published a novel called Futility about a massive, unsinkable ship named the Titan. It hit an iceberg and sank in the North Atlantic. Fourteen years later, the Titanic met the same fate, almost identically.

2011 – Jobs and the Bitten Apple
Fact: When Steve Jobs passed away in 2011, fans left apples with bites

taken out at memorials—completely unaware they were echoing an ancient Greek tradition of placing bitten apples on teachers' graves.

1826 – Founding Fathers Exit Together
Fact: Political rivals turned friends, Thomas Jefferson and John Adams, both died on the same day: July 4, 1826—exactly 50 years after they helped create the Declaration of Independence.

1945 – The Double Survivor
Fact: Tsutomu Yamaguchi survived the atomic bombing of Hiroshima. Three days later, he was in Nagasaki when the second bomb dropped—and survived again.

1891 – Ohio's First Car Crash
Fact: The very first recorded car accident happened in Ohio in 1891, when James Lambert's car hit a tree root and crashed. There were only two cars in the entire state at the time.

1975 – Déjà Vu by Debris
Fact: In 1975, a man died when a piece of debris fell from a skyscraper and hit his taxi. Shockingly, the exact same thing had happened to his brother the year before.

1838/1884 – Richard Parker, Fiction and Flesh
Fact: In 1838, Edgar Allan Poe wrote a story where shipwreck survivors ate a cabin boy named Richard Parker. Decades later, in 1884, real-life shipwreck survivors did the same—also to a boy named Richard Parker.

1979 – The Jim Twins
Fact: Twin brothers Jim Lewis and Jim Springer were separated at birth and reunited at 39, only to discover uncanny similarities: both had dogs named Toy, had married women with the same names, and had sons with the same name.

1920 – Triple Georges on a Train
Fact: In 1920, three men met on a train in Kentucky. They were all named George Phillips, all born on the same day, and all heading to the same convention.

1973 – Hopkins and the Magic Book
Fact: In 1973, actor Anthony Hopkins was cast in The Girl from Petrovka but couldn't find a copy of the novel anywhere. One day, while waiting for a train, he found one lying on a bench. When he later met the author, he learned it was his own annotated copy—lost two years earlier.

1930s – The Baby Catcher of Detroit
Fact: In the 1930s, Detroit street sweeper Joseph Figlock was walking his route when a baby fell from a window. He caught the child, saving its life. Incredibly, the exact same thing happened again—same man, same job, same outcome.

1900 – King Umberto's Twin Twist
Fact: King Umberto I of Italy once dined at a restaurant where the owner looked exactly like him. The man was also named Umberto, born on the same day in the same town. The very next day, both were shot and killed in separate incidents.

1912/1916 – Violet Jessop's Triple Trouble
Fact: Violet Jessop lived through the sinking of the Titanic and its sister ship, the Britannic. She was also aboard their third sibling, the Olympic, when it collided with another vessel—and survived all three incidents.

1861–1865 – The War Bookends of Wilmer McLean
Fact: During the American Civil War, Wilmer McLean moved from Manassas to Appomattox to avoid the chaos. Years later, General Lee surrendered to Grant—in McLean's new living room. He famously said, "The war began in my front yard and ended in my front parlor."

1950s–1980s – Hemingway vs. the FBI
Fact: Ernest Hemingway once told friends he was being followed by the FBI, and they chalked it up to paranoia. But years after his death, declassified documents proved he was right all along.

1883–1913 – The Revenge of the Bullet
Fact: In 1883, Henry Ziegland broke up with his girlfriend, who took her own life shortly after. Her brother, devastated and seeking revenge, shot

Ziegland before turning the gun on himself. But Ziegland survived—the bullet had only grazed his face and lodged in a tree. Years later, Ziegland tried to remove that tree with dynamite. The explosion sent the old bullet flying… and this time, it killed him.

1896 – Speeding at 8 MPH
Fact: The very first person to get a speeding ticket was caught driving 8 mph in a 2 mph zone back in 1896. The officer had to chase him down on a bicycle.

1903/1916 – Spy Story Turned Reality
Fact: Erskine Childers wrote a novel about German spies using a yacht to smuggle weapons for a British invasion. Years later, Childers mirrored his own fiction—he used his yacht to smuggle weapons into Ireland during a rebellion.

1838/1884 – Poe's Premonition: Part II
Fact: In 1838, Edgar Allan Poe published The Narrative of Arthur Gordon Pym, where shipwrecked survivors resort to cannibalism and eat a cabin boy named Richard Parker. In 1884, a real shipwreck occurred—and the survivors ended up eating a cabin boy also named Richard Parker.

1939 – Gadsby and the Vanishing "E"
Fact: The 1939 novel Gadsby by Ernest Vincent Wright is famous for not using the letter "e" even once. Wright died the very day his book was published.

1909 – Titanic Suction Power
Fact: In 1909, a vacuum cleaner ad boasted "Titanic suction power!" alongside an illustration of a sinking ship—three years before the actual Titanic was even built.

1929 – A Childhood Book Comes Home
Fact: In 1929, author Anne Parrish was browsing a bookstore in Paris when she stumbled upon a familiar children's book. Opening it, she found her own name written inside—it was her childhood copy, which had been sold years earlier in New York.

1700s–1800s – Dexter's Dumb Luck

Fact: Timothy Dexter, an eccentric 18th-century businessman, once sent warming pans to the tropical West Indies, where locals used them as molasses dippers—earning him a surprising profit. Encouraged, he sent wool mittens next, which were purchased by a ship heading to chilly Siberia.

1951 – Double Trouble with Dennis the Menace

Fact: On March 12, 1951, Dennis the Menace comic strips were published simultaneously in the US and the UK—created independently by cartoonists who had never heard of each other.

1977–1980s – Agatha Christie Saves Lives

Fact: In 1920, Agatha Christie wrote about a murder involving thallium poisoning. Her description was so accurate that, years later, doctors used the book to diagnose real cases of thallium poisoning.

1930 – No News is... Piano?

Fact: On April 18, 1930, the BBC made an unusual announcement: "There is no news today," and played piano music instead. That same day, a prison guard received an award for going seven years without ever needing to use his keys.

1838/1960 – Ships and Space Dogs

Fact: Back in 1838, the U.S. launched an expedition to Antarctica using two ships: the USS Porpoise and the USS Peacock. Over a century later in 1960, the Soviet Union sent two dogs into space named Belka (squirrel) and Strelka (little arrow)—Russian translations for porpoise and peacock.

1883 – Krakatoa and Krakatoa (Sort Of)

Fact: In 1883, Krakatoa's volcanic eruption produced the loudest sound in recorded history, heard 3,000 miles away. Coincidentally, a composer named Krakatoa Williams had been born in the U.S. just a year earlier.

2012 – Parking Lot Royalty

Fact: In 2012, King Richard III's long-lost remains were discovered buried beneath a parking lot in Leicester—right beneath a spot marked with the letter "R."

1965/1974 – The Lifesaver Cycle

Fact: In 1965, a four-year-old boy was swept out to sea on an Australian beach and rescued by a man named Brian Smith. Nine years later, that same boy saved a drowning man at the same beach. The man? Brian Smith.

1865 – Lightning's Favorite Widow

Fact: In 1865, a lightning bolt struck a portrait of the widow of Confederate general J.E.B. Stuart, damaging everything except her image. On that same day, 90 miles away, another lightning strike hit Stuart's grave.

1800s–San Francisco – Gautier's Fang Fantasy

Fact: French poet Théophile Gautier once joked that he'd one day meet a Chinese man named Fang in California. Years later, while visiting San Francisco, he did—he met a merchant named Fang.

1975–1976 – Taxi Déjà Vu

Fact: In 1975, a man in Bermuda was struck and killed by a taxi. A year earlier, his brother had died in exactly the same way—hit by the same taxi, driven by the same driver, carrying the same passenger, and on the same street.

1838–1847 – The Tale of Santa Anna's Leg

Fact: In 1838, General Antonio López de Santa Anna lost a leg in battle and buried it with full military honors. Years later, during another war, American soldiers dug it up and took it as a war trophy.

1903–1945 – Orville Wright's Full Flight Circle

Fact: Orville Wright, who flew the first powered aircraft in 1903, lived long enough to witness aircraft drop atomic bombs on Hiroshima and Nagasaki in 1945.

1930s–Present – Hoover Dam Still Drying

Fact: The concrete used in the Hoover Dam is so massive, it still hasn't fully cured since it was poured in the 1930s—and won't be fully set for another 500 years.

1913 – Café Central's Historical Bunch
Fact: In 1913, Hitler, Stalin, Trotsky, Tito, and Freud all lived within a few miles of each other in Vienna, often frequenting the same cafés—unknowingly sharing a moment in history.

2002 – Finnish Twins' Fate
Fact: In 2002, a 70-year-old Finnish man was killed crossing a highway. He was hit by a truck—on the exact spot where his twin brother had died two years earlier, in the exact same way.

1909 – Titanic Vacuum Irony
Fact: In 1909, a vacuum cleaner ad boasted "Titanic suction power!" alongside an illustration of a sinking ship—three years before the actual Titanic was even built.

1838 – Richard Parker Redux (Again)
Fact: In 1838, Edgar Allan Poe published The Narrative of Arthur Gordon Pym, where shipwrecked survivors ate a cabin boy named Richard Parker. In 1884, a real shipwreck occurred—and the survivors ate a cabin boy also named Richard Parker.

Unknown – Timothy Dexter's Dumb Luck
Fact: Timothy Dexter, an eccentric 18th-century businessman, once sent warming pans to the tropical West Indies, where locals used them as molasses dippers—earning him a surprising profit. Encouraged, he sent wool mittens next, which were purchased by a ship heading to chilly Siberia.

1929 – Anne Parrish's Parisian Discovery
Fact: In 1929, author Anne Parrish was browsing a bookstore in Paris when she stumbled upon a familiar children's book. Opening it, she found her own name written inside—it was her childhood copy, which had been sold years earlier in New York.

1826 – Presidential Deathday Duo
Fact: Political rivals turned friends, Thomas Jefferson and John Adams,

both died on the same day: July 4, 1826—exactly 50 years after they helped create the Declaration of Independence.

1835 & 1910 – Twain and the Comet
Fact: Mark Twain once predicted he'd go out with Halley's Comet, the same way he came in. And he did—born in 1835 when the comet was visible, and dying in 1910 when it returned.

1898 – The Titan and the Titanic
Fact: In 1898, writer Morgan Robertson published a novel called Futility about a massive, unsinkable ship named the Titan. It hit an iceberg and sank in the North Atlantic. Fourteen years later, the Titanic met the same fate, almost identically.

2011 – Jobs and the Bitten Apple
Fact: When Steve Jobs passed away in 2011, fans left apples with bites taken out at memorials—completely unaware they were echoing an ancient Greek tradition of placing bitten apples on teachers' graves.

1945 – Yamaguchi Survives Twice
Fact: Tsutomu Yamaguchi survived the atomic bombing of Hiroshima. Three days later, he was in Nagasaki when the second bomb dropped—and survived again.

1891 – The First Car Crash
Fact: The very first recorded car accident happened in Ohio in 1891, when James Lambert's car hit a tree root and crashed. There were only two cars in the entire state at the time.

1975 & 1974 – Death by Debris, Twice
Fact: In 1975, a man died when a piece of debris fell from a skyscraper and hit his taxi. Shockingly, the exact same thing had happened to his brother the year before.

1838 & 1884 – Richard Parker Returns (Again)
Fact: In 1838, Edgar Allan Poe wrote a story where shipwreck survivors ate a cabin boy named Richard Parker. Decades later, in 1884, real-life shipwreck survivors did the same—also to a boy named Richard Parker.

Mid-1900s – Twin Jims' Bizarre Lives

Fact: Twin brothers Jim Lewis and Jim Springer were separated at birth and reunited at 39, only to discover uncanny similarities: both had dogs named Toy, had married women with the same names, and had sons with the same name.

1920 – The Three Georges

Fact: In 1920, three men met on a train in Kentucky. They were all named George Phillips, all born on the same day, and all heading to the same convention.

1973 – The Hopkins Book Mystery

Fact: In 1973, actor Anthony Hopkins was cast in The Girl from Petrovka but couldn't find a copy of the novel anywhere. One day, while waiting for a train, he found one lying on a bench. When he later met the author, he learned it was his own annotated copy—lost two years earlier.

1930s – Figlock's Falling Babies

Fact: In the 1930s, Detroit street sweeper Joseph Figlock was walking his route when a baby fell from a window. He caught the child, saving its life. Incredibly, the exact same thing happened again—same man, same job, same outcome.

Late 1800s – Umberto and Umberto

Fact: King Umberto I of Italy once dined at a restaurant where the owner looked exactly like him. The man was also named Umberto, born on the same day in the same town. The very next day, both were shot and killed in separate incidents.

1910s – Violet Jessop, Shipwreck Magnet

Fact: Violet Jessop lived through the sinking of the Titanic and its sister ship, the Britannic. She was also aboard their third sibling, the Olympic, when it collided with another vessel—and survived all three incidents.

1860s – Wilmer McLean and the War That Followed

Fact: During the American Civil War, Wilmer McLean moved from Manassas to Appomattox to avoid the chaos. Years later, General Lee surrendered to Grant—in McLean's new living room. He famously said, "The war began in my front yard and ended in my front parlor."

1950s – Hemingway's FBI Paranoia
Fact: Ernest Hemingway once told friends he was being followed by the FBI, and they chalked it up to paranoia. But years after his death, declassified documents proved he was right all along.

1883–1913 – The Bullet That Waited
Fact: In 1883, Henry Ziegland broke up with his girlfriend, who took her own life shortly after. Her brother shot Ziegland before killing himself. Ziegland survived—the bullet grazed him and lodged in a tree. Years later, when blowing up the tree, the old bullet flew out—and killed him.

1896 – Speed Demon at 8 MPH
Fact: The very first person to get a speeding ticket was caught driving 8 mph in a 2 mph zone back in 1896. The officer had to chase him down on a bicycle.

Early 1900s – Childers and His Fictional Crime
Fact: Erskine Childers wrote a novel about German spies using a yacht to smuggle weapons for a British invasion. Years later, Childers mirrored his own fiction—he used his yacht to smuggle weapons into Ireland during a rebellion.

1838 & 1884 – Richard Parker Revisited Yet Again
Fact: In 1838, Edgar Allan Poe published The Narrative of Arthur Gordon Pym, where shipwrecked survivors eat a cabin boy named Richard Parker. In 1884, real survivors also ate a cabin boy—named Richard Parker.

1939 – The 'E'-less Novel
Fact: The 1939 novel Gadsby by Ernest Vincent Wright is famous for not using the letter "e" even once. Wright died the very day his book was published.

1909 – Titanic Suction Power?
Fact: In 1909, a vacuum cleaner ad boasted "Titanic suction power!"

alongside an illustration of a sinking ship—three years before the actual Titanic was even built.

1929 – Parrish's Paris Book
Fact: In 1929, author Anne Parrish was browsing a bookstore in Paris when she stumbled upon a familiar children's book. Opening it, she found her own name written inside—it was her childhood copy, which had been sold years earlier in New York.

Late 1700s – Dexter's Dumb Luck
Fact: Timothy Dexter, an eccentric 18th-century businessman, once sent warming pans to the tropical West Indies, where locals used them as molasses dippers—earning him a surprising profit. Encouraged, he sent wool mittens next, which were purchased by a ship heading to chilly Siberia.

1951 – Dennis the Menace x2
Fact: On March 12, 1951, Dennis the Menace comic strips were published simultaneously in the US and the UK—created independently by cartoonists who had never heard of each other.

1970s – Christie's Clue Saves Lives
Fact: In 1920, Agatha Christie wrote about a murder involving thallium poisoning. Her description was so accurate that, years later, doctors used the book to diagnose real cases of thallium poisoning.

1930 – No News Day
Fact: On April 18, 1930, the BBC made an unusual announcement: "There is no news today," and played piano music instead. That same day, a prison guard received an award for going seven years without ever needing to use his keys.

1838 & 1960 – Porpoise, Peacock &... Pups?
Fact: Back in 1838, the U.S. launched an expedition to Antarctica using two ships: the USS Porpoise and the USS Peacock. Over a century later in 1960, the Soviet Union sent two dogs into space named Belka (squirrel) and Strelka (little arrow)—Russian translations for porpoise and peacock.

1883 – Krakatoa and Krakatoa
Fact: In 1883, Krakatoa's volcanic eruption produced the loudest sound in recorded history, heard 3,000 miles away. Coincidentally, a composer named Krakatoa Williams had been born in the U.S. just a year earlier.

2012 – R for Richard
Fact: In 2012, King Richard III's long-lost remains were discovered buried beneath a parking lot in Leicester—right beneath a spot marked with the letter "R."

1965–1974 – Beach Rescue Déjà Vu
Fact: In 1965, a four-year-old boy was swept out to sea on an Australian beach and rescued by a man named Brian Smith. Nine years later, that same boy saved a drowning man at the same beach. The man? Brian Smith.

1865 – Lightning and the Widow's Portrait
Fact: In 1865, a lightning bolt struck a portrait of the widow of Confederate general J.E.B. Stuart, damaging everything except her image. On that same day, 90 miles away, another lightning strike hit Stuart's grave.

1800s – Gautier and Fang
Fact: French poet Théophile Gautier once joked that he'd one day meet a Chinese man named Fang in California. Years later, while visiting San Francisco, he did—he met a merchant named Fang.

1975 – Taxi Tragedy Times Two
Fact: In 1975, a man in Bermuda was struck and killed by a taxi. A year earlier, his brother had died in exactly the same way—hit by the same taxi, driven by the same driver, carrying the same passenger, and on the same street.

1838–1847 – Santa Anna's Lost Leg
Fact: In 1838, General Antonio López de Santa Anna lost a leg in battle and buried it with full military honors. Years later, during another war, American soldiers dug it up and took it as a war trophy.

1903–1945 – Orville's Flight to Fallout
Fact: Orville Wright, who flew the first powered aircraft in 1903, lived

long enough to witness aircraft drop atomic bombs on Hiroshima and Nagasaki in 1945.

1930s–2500s – Curing the Dam
Fact: The concrete used in the Hoover Dam is so massive, it still hasn't fully cured since it was poured in the 1930s—and won't be fully set for another 500 years.

1913 – Café of Giants
Fact: In 1913, Hitler, Stalin, Trotsky, Tito, and Freud all lived within a few miles of each other in Vienna, often frequenting the same cafés—unknowingly sharing a moment in history.

2002 – Twin Tragedy
Fact: In 2002, a 70-year-old Finnish man was killed crossing a highway. He was hit by a truck—on the exact spot where his twin brother had died two years earlier, in the exact same way.

🚽 Flush-Worthy Firsts"

#1 🚽 **First medieval "employee benefit"?** — 14th century England. Gong farmers (the guys who cleaned cesspits) were paid more than teachers.

#2 🚽 **First confirmed skydiver… without a parachute?** — 1912. Franz Reichelt jumped off the Eiffel Tower testing his invention. It did not go well.

#3 🚽 **First spam message?** — 1864. A dentist sent unsolicited telegrams to London residents. The only drill involved was marketing.

#4 🚽 **First Olympic scandal?** — 1904. Marathon winner Fred Lorz hitched a ride in a car for part of the race. Disqualified for obvious reasons.

#5 🚽 **First vending machine?** — Ancient Greece. Hero of Alexandria created one that dispensed holy water. Insert coin, get sacred splash.

17. Unusual Punishments Throughout the Ages

Medieval England – Bad Beer, Brutal Bridle
Fact: Brewers who sold bad beer could be punished by wearing the scold's bridle—a metal mask that clamped their mouth shut. A literal taste of their own medicine... denied.

Ancient China – Theatre of Shame
Fact: Corrupt officials during the Zhou Dynasty were forced to watch plays mocking their crimes. Justice took center stage   humiliation was the ticket price.

17th-Century New England – Clothespin Justice
Fact: Gossip too much in Puritan New England, and you might end up with clothespins on your tongue. Painful, silencing, and definitely not small talk-friendly.

Tudor England – Nailed for Skipping Church
Fact: Skip church in Tudor England and you could be nailed to the door—

by your ear. The only escape? Rip yourself free. Sunday service suddenly seemed more appealing.

Ancient Rome – The Sack of Doom
Fact: Parricide was punished by sewing the killer into a sack with a dog, monkey, rooster, and viper—then tossing it into a river. Roman justice didn't do subtle.

Medieval Germany – Dunk the Dishonest Baker
Fact: Bakers who cheated customers with light loaves were dunked in a pond—publicly and repeatedly. Wet, cold, and well deserved.

Colonial America – Vegetable-Fueled Shame Solo
Fact: Bad musicians in early America were made to perform in public while people pelted them with vegetables. Rough reviews were delivered produce-first.

Ancient Persia – The Boats of Horror
Fact: Victims were fed milk and honey, smeared in more honey, then left between boats to be eaten alive by bugs. Persian execution... slow and sticky.

Spanish Inquisition – The Strappado Slam
Fact: Tied hands, hoisted up, dropped hard—but stopped short of the ground. Joints popped, confessions followed, and the floor remained teasingly out of reach.

Mongol Empire – No Noble Bloodshed
Fact: Mongol nobles sentenced to death were wrapped in carpets and trampled by horses. It preserved their blood—and shattered their bones.

16th-Century Scotland – Tongue-Tied by Fire
Fact: Blasphemers in Scotland had their tongues pierced with hot irons—an excruciating way to say "watch your mouth." Speech was still possible… just not preferred.

Colonial America – Backward Husband Parade
Fact: Submissive husbands were punished by being paraded through town

on a donkey—backward and dressed in women's clothing. Patriarchy wasn't amused.

Medieval Germany – Barrel of Shame
Fact: Poor performers were shoved into barrels with only their heads sticking out and paraded around. It was music criticism—medieval style.

Ancient China – Facial Ink of Shame
Fact: Criminals had their crimes tattooed onto their faces, permanently marking them for society. Face it—your past literally followed you.

Colonial America – The Ducking Stool
Fact: "Scolds," or overly talkative women, were tied to chairs and dunked repeatedly into rivers. Public silence, enforced by splashes.

Viking Scandinavia – Outlawed by Honor
Fact: Oath-breakers were declared "nithing"—honorless and killable by anyone, no legal consequences. The Norse took their promises seriously.

Medieval Europe – Hands Off the Dice
Fact: Cheating at dice or cards could get your hand stabbed into the table with a dagger. Nothing says "don't cheat" like blood-stained gaming.

Ancient Rome – Drink What You Tried to Steal
Fact: Caught stealing books? Romans might force you to drink ink—a literary punishment, taken quite literally.

Medieval Islamic Middle East – The Backward Ride of Shame
Fact: Corrupt officials rode donkeys backward through town, wearing signs detailing their crimes. Justice by humiliation—no gallows required.

Ancient Babylon – False Accuser's Fate
Fact: Make a false accusation in Babylon, and you received the punishment you wished on someone else. Justice wasn't blind—it was vengeful.

🚽 Punishment or Performance?

Think you've got what it takes to survive history's weirdest justice systems? Match each punishment below with its historical origin. No cheating—unless you're prepared to have your hand pinned to the table.

1. Tattooed with your crimes
2. Forced to drink ink
3. Thrown into a sack with wild animals
4. Paraded in a barrel with only your head showing
5. Dunked repeatedly for gossiping
6. Tongue pierced with hot irons
7. Watched plays mocking your crimes

A. Ancient China
B. Ancient Rome
C. Medieval Germany
D. 16th-century Scotland
E. Colonial America
F. Zhou Dynasty China
G. Ancient Rome (again!)

Answers:

1–A, 2–G, 3–B, 4–C, 5–E, 6–D, 7–F

18. Strange Origin of Everyday Phrases

16th Century – Sleep Tight

Fact: The phrase "sleep tight" dates back to the 16th century, when mattresses were supported by ropes. To keep the bed firm and comfortable, those ropes had to be tightened regularly—hence, "sleep tight."

1800s – Saved by the Bell

Fact: "Saved by the bell" has its roots in the 1800s, when fears of being buried alive led to a chilling invention: strings were tied to the wrists of the recently buried, connected to bells above ground. If someone was mistakenly declared dead, the bell could signal their desperate call for help.

1600s – Burning the Midnight Oil

Fact: "Burning the midnight oil" comes from the 1600s, a time when people relied on oil lamps to work late into the night. If you stayed up working, you were literally burning oil past midnight.

1800s – Mad as a Hatter

Fact: The phrase "mad as a hatter" took shape in the 1800s, when hat makers used mercury in the felting process. Prolonged exposure caused serious neurological damage, leading to tremors, confusion, and erratic behavior—thus, the hatter's madness.

Ancient Egypt – Cat Got Your Tongue?
Fact: "Cat got your tongue?" might trace back to ancient Egypt, where it's said that the tongues of liars and blasphemers were cut out and fed to cats. Though the origin is debated, the phrase still hints at a silencing fear.

English Law (Disputed) – Rule of Thumb
Fact: The expression "rule of thumb" is believed by some to come from an old English law that allowed a man to beat his wife with a stick no thicker than his thumb. While historians question the accuracy of this claim, the grim association has stuck with the phrase.

Medieval England – Giving the Cold Shoulder
Fact: "Giving the cold shoulder" began in medieval England, when a host wanted to signal that a guest had overstayed their welcome. Instead of a warm meal, they were served a cold shoulder of mutton—a subtle way of saying it was time to go.

17th Century – Raining Cats and Dogs
Fact: The phrase "raining cats and dogs" likely traces back to 17th-century England. During heavy storms, gutters would overflow and sometimes wash away the bodies of dead animals from rooftops and streets, making it look as though they'd fallen from the sky.

Victorian England – Pulling Someone's Leg
Fact: "Pulling someone's leg" began in Victorian England, where thieves had a literal trick up their sleeve. They would trip victims using a wire or stick to make them fall, making it easier to rob them.

1800s – Bite the Bullet
Fact: "Bite the bullet" comes from 1800s battlefield medicine. In the absence of anesthesia, wounded soldiers were given bullets to bite down on during surgery to help endure the pain.

1800s – Dead Ringer
Fact: The term "dead ringer" emerged in the 1800s out of a very real fear

of being buried alive. Some coffins were rigged with strings attached to bells above ground, so if someone was mistakenly buried, they could ring for help.

14th Century – Eat Humble Pie
Fact: To "eat humble pie" comes from the older "umble pie," a dish made from the innards of deer. In the 14th century, it was typically served to servants and the lower classes—eating it symbolized accepting a lower status or admitting fault.

World War II Era – Go the Whole Nine Yards
Fact: "Go the whole nine yards" may date back to World War II. Fighter pilots' machine gun belts were nine yards long, so using the full belt in combat meant giving it everything you had.

17th Century – Mind Your P's and Q's
Fact: "Mind your P's and Q's" likely started in 17th-century English pubs, where bartenders kept track of how much people drank by marking their pints and quarts on a chalkboard—reminding customers to mind their manners and their tabs.

1801 – Turn a Blind Eye
Fact: "Turn a blind eye" comes from a bold act by Admiral Horatio Nelson in 1801. During the Battle of Copenhagen, when ordered to retreat, he famously raised his telescope to his blind eye—pretending not to see the signal and continuing the attack.

13th Century – Baker's Dozen
Fact: A "baker's dozen" dates back to 13th-century England, when strict laws punished bakers for selling underweight bread. To avoid penalties, bakers would add an extra item to make sure they met the standard—thirteen instead of twelve.

Biblical/Medieval – Blood is Thicker Than Water (Full Phrase)
Fact: "Blood is thicker than water" originally meant the opposite of how we use it today. The full saying was "the blood of the covenant is thicker

than the water of the womb," suggesting that bonds formed by choice could be stronger than those of family.

15th Century – Caught Red-Handed
Fact: The phrase "caught red-handed" comes from 15th-century Scotland, where poachers were often found with blood still on their hands after killing animals illegally—making their guilt unmistakable.

Nautical – Break the Ice
Fact: "Break the ice" has nautical roots. When large ships were blocked by frozen waters, smaller boats called "ice-breakers" were sent ahead to clear a path, allowing safe passage. The phrase came to mean making the first move to ease tension in a situation.

Ancient Greece – Spill the Beans
Fact: "Spill the beans" dates back to ancient Greece, where votes were cast using beans placed in jars. If the jar tipped or the beans were spilled too early, the results would be revealed before the official count.

Ancient Folklore – Hair of the Dog
Fact: "Hair of the dog" originally referred to an old belief that the hair from the dog that bit you could be used as a remedy for the wound. By the 1500s, the phrase had taken on a new meaning—using alcohol to treat a hangover caused by alcohol.

17th Century – Pleased as Punch
Fact: "Pleased as punch" comes from the puppet character Mr. Punch, who was always gleeful—especially after acts of mischief or violence in the popular 17th-century Punch and Judy shows.

1920s – Jaywalking
Fact: "Jaywalking" emerged in the 1920s, when "jay" was a slang term for someone naïve or from the countryside. These folks were unfamiliar with city traffic laws and would often cross streets carelessly.

Horse Trading Era – Straight from the Horse's Mouth
Fact: "Straight from the horse's mouth" refers to how buyers checked a horse's teeth to determine its age and health—information you couldn't

fake. Hearing it "from the horse's mouth" meant getting it straight from the most reliable source.

Children's Games – Upper Hand

Fact: "Upper hand" began with children's stick-grabbing games, where players took turns placing hands above each other on a stick. The one who reached the top—or got the upper hand—won.

Frontier America – Passing the Buck

Fact: "Passing the buck" comes from frontier poker games in the 1800s. A buckhorn-handled knife was used to mark whose turn it was to deal. When a player didn't want the responsibility, they'd pass the knife—thus, "passing the buck."

WWII Era – Bought the Farm

Fact: "Bought the farm" originated during World War II. When a soldier died in service, the compensation given to their family was often just enough to pay off their mortgage—symbolically, they had "bought the farm."

Feudal England – Windfall

Fact: "Windfall" goes back to feudal England, where commoners were banned from chopping down trees. However, if wood fell due to a storm, they were allowed to collect it. These unexpected gains were called "windfalls."

1500s Europe – Don't Throw the Baby Out with the Bathwater

Fact: "Don't throw the baby out with the bathwater" comes from 1500s Europe, when families reused bathwater. The baby was bathed last, often in water so murky that someone might genuinely risk tossing out the baby with it.

Early 1900s – Put a Sock in It

Fact: "Put a sock in it" dates to early phonographs, which had no volume controls. To lower the sound, people would literally stuff a sock into the speaker horn.

1714 – Read the Riot Act
Fact: "Read the riot act" comes from the Riot Act of 1714 in Britain. Before authorities could disperse a group of twelve or more people, they had to read a specific proclamation aloud. Only then could legal action be taken.

1800s – Fly Off the Handle
Fact: "Fly off the handle" refers to poorly made axes in the 1800s. If the head flew off while in use, it could cause serious harm—just like someone suddenly losing their temper.

Sailing Slang – Three Sheets to the Wind
Fact: "Three sheets to the wind" is a sailing term from the 1800s. Sheets are ropes that control sails. If three were loose, the ship would lurch uncontrollably—like a drunken sailor.

Ancient India – To Butter Someone Up
Fact: "To butter someone up" has roots in ancient India, where people would toss butter at statues of gods as an offering to gain favor. The idea stuck—today it means flattering someone to get what you want.

12th-Century England – Bringing Home the Bacon
Fact: "Bringing home the bacon" may come from a 12th-century tradition in Great Dunmow, England. Couples who could prove they hadn't argued for a year were rewarded with a side of bacon—a prize for harmony at home.

1704 – Steal One's Thunder
Fact: "Steal one's thunder" came from 1704, when playwright John Dennis invented a new way to mimic thunder on stage. After his play flopped, he discovered other productions had adopted his technique—without credit.

Execution Traditions – On the Wagon
Fact: "On the wagon" refers to prisoners being carted to execution. They were allowed a final drink unless they refused it—those who did were said to be "on the wagon," abstaining from alcohol.

1800s Mexico – The Whole Enchilada

Fact: "The whole enchilada" came into English slang in the 1960s but traces back to a Mexican phrase from the 1800s: "todo el enchilado," referring to the whole thing—complete and undivided.

Ancient Rome – Get Up on the Wrong Side of the Bed

Fact: "Get up on the wrong side of the bed" goes all the way back to ancient Rome, where stepping out of bed on the left side was thought to bring bad luck. That superstition eventually led to our modern take on grumpy mornings.

Siam (Thailand) – White Elephant

Fact: "White elephant" comes from Siam, now Thailand. Albino elephants were considered sacred and could not be put to work. When the king wanted to punish a courtier subtly, he'd gift them one—an honor that came with unbearable expense.

🚽 "Say What?" – Phrase Origins Trivia Challenge

Match the weird phrase to its origin:
1. Read the riot act
2. Three sheets to the wind
3. White elephant
4. Bring home the bacon
5. Butter someone up

A. Ancient Indian butter offerings
B. Sacred gift from a king in Siam
C. Sailors with loose ropes = drunken wobble
D. English prize for peaceful couples
E. British law to control unruly mobs

Answers:

1-E, 2-C, 3-B, 4-D, 5-A

19. Absurd Laws That Once Existed

England, 17th Century – No Armor in Parliament
Fact: In 17th-century England, wearing armor in Parliament was illegal. The rule aimed to prevent violence during heated debates and—technically—remains law, just in case a knight tries storming in.

Minneapolis, 1973 – Romantic Deception Law
Fact: Until 1973, men in Minneapolis could face jail time for seducing unmarried women through deception. Aimed at protecting women's reputations, it sounds like the plot of a courtroom soap opera.

Massachusetts, 1799 – Mandatory Christmas?
Fact: A rumor claims George Washington signed a law making it illegal *not* to celebrate Christmas in Massachusetts. More myth than mandate, but it reflects how serious folks were about holiday cheer.

France, 1800–2013 – Women and Trousers
Fact: For over 200 years, French women needed official permission to wear pants—unless riding a horse or bicycle. The law, meant to preserve "public decency," wasn't repealed until 2013.

England, Victorian Era – Betting on the PM
Fact: In Victorian England, it was illegal to bet on the Prime Minister's death. Offenders faced hard labor—because apparently, death pools weren't considered very classy.

Canada, 1837–1921 – Education Comes at a Cost
Fact: Indigenous Canadians who earned university degrees lost their legal Indian status. This harsh policy was part of colonial assimilation efforts that punished education with cultural erasure.

Turkey, 16th Century – Death for Drinking Coffee
Fact: Sultan Murad IV banned coffee in 16th-century Turkey, believing it brewed rebellion. Violators weren't just fined—they risked execution for a cup of joe.

England, 1313–1960 – Sunday Archery Practice
Fact: A medieval law required all English males over 14 to practice archery for two hours every Sunday. It wasn't officially repealed until 1960, just in case the longbow made a comeback.

New Jersey, Colonial Era – Leap Year Proposals
Fact: In colonial America, New Jersey passed a law making it illegal for men to refuse marriage proposals from unmarried women during leap years. A man who declined could be fined £5 for "breach of promise."

Singapore, 1942–1957 – The Great Gum Ban
Fact: From 1942 to 1957, chewing gum was banned in Singapore due to concerns about public cleanliness and improper disposal.

Indiana, 1897 – Pi = 3.2?
Fact: In 1897, the Indiana state legislature attempted to pass a bill that would legally define the value of pi as exactly 3.2. The measure was stopped after a mathematician intervened to explain the mathematical error.

England, 1313–2000 – Longbow Sundays (Yes, Still)
Fact: Until the year 2000, a 1313 English law technically required all men over the age of 14 to practice longbow archery for two hours each week under the supervision of their parish clergy.

Rome, c. 200 BCE – No Gold for Women
Fact: In Ancient Rome, around 200 BCE, the Oppian Law restricted women from owning more than half an ounce of gold and from wearing multi-colored garments, especially purple, which was associated with wealth and power.

England, 16th Century – Dress Code by Class
Fact: In 16th-century England, the Sumptuary Laws regulated clothing based on social class. These laws dictated which colors and fabrics individuals could wear according to their status and income.

USA, 1919–1933 – Prohibition Loopholes
Fact: Between 1919 and 1930, Prohibition in the United States made it illegal to manufacture, transport, or sell alcoholic beverages. However, the law allowed homeowners to produce up to 200 gallons of wine per year for personal use.

Prussia, 18th Century – Coffee for the Elite Only
Fact: In 18th-century Prussia, Frederick the Great banned the consumption of coffee among commoners, reserving it for the nobility. Officials known as "coffee sniffers" were employed to detect and prevent illegal brewing.

London, 1908–1980 – No Lunch While Driving
Fact: From 1908 to 1980, Londoners were technically prohibited from hailing a taxi if the cab driver was eating his lunch.

England, 1649 – The War on Christmas
Fact: In 1649, Oliver Cromwell's Puritan government banned Christmas celebrations in England. The holiday was viewed as too indulgent and pagan, and soldiers were sent to patrol the streets and confiscate food being prepared for Christmas feasts.

England, 1700s – Wife for Sale (With Consent)
Fact: Until the late 1700s in England, a husband could legally sell his wife at market. If the sale was conducted publicly and with her consent, it was considered a binding form of divorce.

Alabama, 1950s – No Confetti for You

Fact: In the 1950s, it was illegal in Mobile, Alabama, to throw confetti or spray silly string during Mardi Gras. Violators could face a $100 fine.

Scotland, 15th Century – Golf Banned (Seriously)

Fact: In 15th-century Scotland, playing golf was banned because it was believed to distract men from archery practice, which was essential for military readiness.

Holy Roman Empire, 16th Century – Shoe Size by Status

Fact: In the Holy Roman Empire during the 16th century, a man's social status determined the legal length of his shoes. A prince could wear shoes up to 30 inches long, while a common knight was limited to 18 inches.

China, 618–907 CE – No Birthmark Bureaucrats

Fact: During the Tang Dynasty in China (618–907 CE), individuals with dragon-shaped birthmarks were banned from holding public office, as such marks were believed to signify imperial descent.

England, Medieval Period – No Swan for You

Fact: In medieval England, commoners were not allowed to eat swans. The birds were considered royal property and were reserved for the monarchy.

Vermont, Early 20th Century – Husband Required for Toothache

Fact: In early 20th-century Vermont, a woman needed her husband's permission to get her teeth fixed, even if she was experiencing pain.

USA, 1799 – Don't Freelance Diplomacy

Fact: In 1799, President John Adams signed the Logan Act into law, making it illegal for unauthorized citizens to negotiate with foreign governments. The law is still technically in effect, though it has only led to one indictment and no convictions.

England, 1530s – Mandatory Hats for Men

Fact: Under King Henry VIII in the 1530s, English men were legally required to wear hats in public. Those who failed to comply could be fined.

UK, Until 1967 – Suicide Was a Crime

Fact: Until 1967, it was illegal in the United Kingdom to attempt suicide. Individuals who survived could face prison time.

Japan, 9th Century – Purple Reserved for Elites

Fact: In 9th-century Japan, only high-ranking courtiers were allowed to wear purple clothing. Violating this law could result in a death sentence.

New England, 1639 – Toasting Banned

Fact: In colonial New England, a 1639 law banned the practice of drinking toasts, which was believed to encourage excessive alcohol consumption.

England, 1439 – No Smooching Allowed

Fact: In 1439, King Henry VI of England banned kissing to prevent the spread of the plague. Violators could face legal penalties.

China, 1368–1644 – Course Limits at Dinner Parties

Fact: During the Ming Dynasty in China, the number of courses at dinner parties was legally limited based on the rank of the highest-status guest present.

Spain, 18th Century – Makeup for Registered Ladies Only

Fact: In 18th-century Spain, only registered prostitutes were legally allowed to wear makeup. Cosmetics were associated with immorality, and others were barred from their use.

UK, Until 1960 – Stamp Orientation Treason

Fact: Until 1960, British law made it illegal to mail a letter unless the stamp with the monarch's image faced outward on the envelope. Turning the image inward was considered an act of treason.

England, 1543–1951 – No Summoning Spirits

Fact: A law passed in 1543 during the Tudor era made it illegal to predict the future by "conjuring spirits." This law technically remained in effect until 1951.

Japan, 1603–1867 – No Public Sushi for Commoners

Fact: During Japan's Edo period, commoners were banned from eating sushi in public. It was considered a luxury meant only for the elite.

USA, 1942–1944 – Ban on Pre-Sliced Bread
Fact: From 1942 to 1944, the U.S. War Production Board banned the sale of pre-sliced bread as a wartime conservation measure. The goal was to save wax paper and reduce wear on bakery equipment.

England, 1533 – Seven-Year Rule for Apprentices
Fact: In 1533, Henry VIII introduced a law requiring apprentices to serve seven years before they could legally be recognized as craftsmen.

Venice, 18th Century – Debtor's Shame Seat
Fact: In 18th-century Venice, gamblers who could not pay their debts at the Ridotto casino were forced by law to sit on the "stone of shame" in St. Mark's Square, where they were exposed to public ridicule.

Virginia, 1671 – Pig Laws and Prejudice
Fact: A 1671 law in Virginia prohibited Native Americans and Black individuals from keeping pigs unless they were confined. In contrast, pigs owned by white colonists were allowed to roam freely.

🚽 Law or LOL?

Can you guess which of these laws were real and which were just totally made up by history pranksters?
(Answers at the bottom—but no peeking until you've committed!)

1. It was illegal in Florida to sing while wearing a swimsuit.
2. In Switzerland, it's against the law to flush a toilet after 10 PM in an apartment.
3. In medieval France, pigs were tried in court and sometimes executed for crimes.
4. In 1950s America, it was illegal to whistle while walking backwards on a Sunday.
5. In Samoa, it's illegal to forget your wife's birthday.

Answers:

1. *Real-ish!* This was debated and joked about in Florida for years, though enforcement is practically nonexistent.

2. *True!* Some apartment buildings in Switzerland have strict quiet hours, and flushing late at night has been regulated.

3. *Absolutely real.* Pigs, rats, and even locusts faced trials in bizarre medieval European courts.

4. *Totally made up.* But let's be honest—someone's probably tried.

5. *True in spirit!* While not strictly enforced, forgetting your wife's birthday can result in legal trouble under Samoa's domestic dispute laws.

20. Historical Scandals That Made Headlines

1814 – The London Beer Flood
Fact: A massive vat exploded at Meux's Brewery, unleashing over 320,000 gallons of beer into London streets. Homes were destroyed, basements flooded, and eight people drowned in what remains one of the strangest industrial disasters ever.

1922 – Hollywood's Unsolved Murder
Fact: Famed director William Desmond Taylor was found murdered in his bungalow. Despite media frenzy and a list of celebrity suspects, the case remains unsolved to this day.

1982 – The Tylenol Poisonings
Fact: Seven people died after ingesting cyanide-laced Tylenol capsules. The random, horrifying attacks led to nationwide panic and the birth of tamper-proof packaging in the pharmaceutical industry.

1957 – The Quiz Show Scandal
Fact: Charles Van Doren shocked the nation by admitting he was fed

answers on the hit show *Twenty-One*. The scandal exposed TV manipulation and ended quiz shows' golden age.

1869 – Black Friday Gold Panic
Fact: Jay Gould and Jim Fisk tried to corner the gold market, but when their scheme collapsed, the economy took a hit. It became a textbook case of greed-fueled chaos.

1923 – Teapot Dome Scandal Returns
Fact: Interior Secretary Albert Fall secretly leased oil reserves for bribes. The fallout was so huge, Fall became the first U.S. Cabinet member to serve prison time.

1882 – The Trial of Charles Guiteau
Fact: James Garfield's assassin, Charles Guiteau, claimed divine motivation during his trial. His bizarre behavior fascinated the public before he was hanged for his crime.

1972 – The Bobby Fischer Chess Meltdown
Fact: In a Cold War showdown, Bobby Fischer's paranoia, demands, and tantrums made the 1972 Chess Championship as much soap opera as sport—and unforgettable.

1987 – Iran-Contra Affair
Fact: The Reagan administration secretly sold arms to Iran and funneled the money to Nicaraguan rebels—violating U.S. law. The scandal sparked investigations and trust issues that lingered for years.

2003 – Jayson Blair and the New York Times
Fact: Rising journalist Jayson Blair was caught fabricating and plagiarizing stories. The fallout rocked the New York Times and led to major reforms in newsroom accountability.

1974 – Patty Hearst Kidnapping
Fact: Heiress Patty Hearst was abducted by a radical group and soon appeared helping them rob a bank. Her transformation from victim to armed accomplice sparked debates over brainwashing and criminal accountability.

2015 – Volkswagen Emissions Scandal

Fact: VW admitted to cheating emissions tests using secret software in millions of vehicles. The scandal damaged its eco-friendly image and cost the company billions in fines and lawsuits.

1940s–1950s – The Hollywood Blacklist

Fact: Suspected communists in Hollywood were banned from working during the Red Scare. Many talented artists lost their careers—some forced to write under fake names to survive.

1969 – Chappaquiddick Incident

Fact: Ted Kennedy drove off a bridge, causing the death of Mary Jo Kopechne. His delayed response and vague explanations ignited public outrage and haunted his political future.

1981 – Prince Charles and Lady Diana's Tumultuous Marriage

Fact: The fairy tale wedding turned tragic as infidelity, emotional distance, and intense media pressure tore their marriage apart—leading to a very public and painful divorce in 1996.

2001 – Enron Collapse

Fact: Enron hid massive debts using shady accounting tricks. When the truth emerged, it triggered one of the biggest corporate collapses in history—wiping out billions and public trust.

2009 – Tiger Woods' Public Unraveling

Fact: A car crash outside Tiger's home uncovered a web of affairs, shattering his clean image. Sponsors fled, his game declined, and the tabloids had a field day.

1989 – Pete Rose Banned from Baseball

Fact: Baseball's hit king was permanently banned for betting on games while managing. Despite his record-breaking stats, he remains locked out of the Hall of Fame.

2013 – Edward Snowden's NSA Leaks

Fact: Snowden leaked top-secret files revealing massive government surveillance programs. Branded a hero by some, traitor by others, he remains in exile as privacy debates rage on.

2006 – Pluto Gets Demoted

Fact: Scientists voted to strip Pluto of its planetary status, sparking public outcry. The technical reason didn't matter—people just didn't want to say goodbye to their favorite little planet.

1993 – Michael Jackson Allegations Begin

Fact: The King of Pop faced his first child abuse allegation in 1993. Though settled out of court, the accusation permanently altered his public image and trailed him for years.

🚽 Bathroom Trivia: Scandal Edition

Ready to flush out the truth from history's dirtiest details? Let's see how scandal-savvy you really are!

#1. What brought down U.S. President Richard Nixon in 1974?

☐ A) He was caught eating pudding with a fork

☐ B) A break-in at the Democratic National Committee headquarters

☐ C) He tried to outlaw disco

☐ D) He got lost in the White House basement

#2. Which royal gave up the throne for love?

☐ A) King Arthur   ☐ C) Prince Harry

☐ B) King Edward VIII   ☐ D) King of Popcorn

#3. What did the "Teapot Dome Scandal" involve?

☐ A) Smuggling teapots

☐ B) Leaking royal gossip

☐ C) Illegally leasing federal oil reserves

☐ D) Spilling tea at the actual dome

#4. What was the bizarre cause of the 1919 Boston tragedy that killed 21 people?

☐ A) Flaming bagpipes

☐ B) A molasses tank explosion

☐ C) Too much tea

☐ D) The Great Toilet Paper Panic

#5. Who was the president involved in the Monica Lewinsky scandal?

☐ A) George Washington ☐ C) Bill Clinton

☐ B) Abraham Lincoln ☐ D) Captain Crunch

Answers:

1–B, 2–B, 3–C, 4–B, 5–C

21. Unexpected Inventions That Shaped the World

1928 – Penicillin
Fact: After returning from vacation, Alexander Fleming found a mold in one of his petri dishes killing the surrounding bacteria. That accidental discovery led to penicillin—the first true antibiotic that revolutionized medicine.

1945 – The Microwave Oven
Fact: While working with radar, Percy Spencer noticed a chocolate bar in his pocket had melted. Intrigued, he experimented further and realized microwaves could cook food—leading to the invention of the microwave oven.

1942 – The Slinky
Fact: Naval engineer Richard James accidentally knocked over a spring and watched it "walk" across the floor. That moment of playful surprise led to the creation of the Slinky, one of the world's most iconic toys.

1886 – Coca-Cola
Fact: Coca-Cola was invented by pharmacist John Pemberton as a headache remedy and a cure for morphine addiction. The original recipe included both cocaine and caffeine—quite different from the fizzy drink we know today.

1853 – Potato Chips
Fact: Chef George Crum, irritated by a fussy customer, sliced potatoes paper-thin and fried them until crisp. His petty revenge turned into one of the most popular snack foods ever—potato chips.

1968 – Post-it Notes
Fact: 3M scientist Spencer Silver created a weak adhesive no one knew how to use. Years later, his colleague Art Fry used it to mark pages in his hymnal, and Post-it Notes quietly became an office staple.

1956 – The Pacemaker
Fact: While building a heart recording device, Wilson Greatbatch used the wrong resistor. Instead of recording, the circuit pulsed like a heartbeat—accidentally creating the first implantable pacemaker.

1903 – Tea Bags
Fact: Thomas Sullivan sent tea samples in silk bags, and customers assumed the bags were meant to be steeped whole. Without meaning to, they brewed up the idea for the modern tea bag.

1953 – WD-40
Fact: The Rocket Chemical Company spent 39 failed attempts trying to develop a rust-prevention formula. Success came on the 40th try—hence the name "Water Displacement, 40th formula."

1888 – Pneumatic Tires
Fact: John Dunlop wanted to make his son's tricycle ride smoother, so he invented a rubber tire filled with air. That simple idea sparked a revolution in transportation—paving the way for modern wheels.

1932–1958 – LEGO Bricks
Fact: Danish carpenter Ole Kirk Christiansen began making wooden toys

in 1932, later switching to plastic. By 1958, he had perfected the interlocking brick design—giving the world LEGO as we know it.

1895 – X-Rays
Fact: Wilhelm Röntgen noticed a nearby screen glowing while experimenting with cathode rays. Though the tube was covered, something invisible was passing through—he had just discovered X-rays.

1879 – Saccharin
Fact: Chemist Constantin Fahlberg forgot to wash his hands after working in the lab. Later at dinner, he noticed his bread tasted oddly sweet—and realized he'd accidentally discovered saccharin.

1780 – The Chainsaw
Fact: The chainsaw was originally invented as a surgical tool for cutting bone during childbirth. Powered by a hand crank, it looked more like a torture device than something you'd take camping.

1942 – Superglue
Fact: While trying to develop clear plastic for gun sights, Dr. Harry Coover stumbled upon a glue that stuck to everything. Too sticky to use in war—it later became the perfect household fix-it tool.

1912 – Stainless Steel
Fact: Harry Brearley was trying to make better gun barrels when he noticed a discarded metal didn't rust. That stainless steel alloy ended up revolutionizing cutlery, cookware, and everything shiny.

1945 – The Giant Microwave
Fact: Percy Spencer's chocolate-bar incident didn't just lead to the microwave oven—it led to a monster-sized one. The first microwave was over 5 feet tall and weighed 750 pounds!

1957 – Bubble Wrap Wallpaper
Fact: Engineers tried to market bubble wrap as textured wallpaper, then greenhouse insulation. Neither idea stuck—but it eventually found its true calling as everyone's favorite packaging (and stress relief).

1943 – The Slinky
Fact: In another version of the story, the Slinky was born when Richard James watched a spring "walk" down some books. Whether shelf or stack, the accidental toy was an instant hit.

1989 – Viagra
Fact: Originally tested as a heart medication, Viagra's *other* effects were so noticeable that test subjects didn't want to return the pills. Pfizer wisely pivoted—and made pharmaceutical history.

1930s – Play-Doh's Soapy Origins
Fact: Play-Doh was first made to clean wallpaper. When coal heating declined, so did dirty walls—so the product got repackaged as a kids' toy. Clean mistake, brilliant pivot.

1928 – Penicillin
Fact: Once more for the mold in the room—Alexander Fleming returned from vacation to find bacteria mysteriously dying in a petri dish. That fungus turned out to be penicillin, changing medicine forever.

1956 – Pacemaker, Round Two
Fact: Wilson Greatbatch's famous resistor mishap sparked (literally) the idea for the implantable pacemaker. One small mistake, one giant leap for cardiac care.

1895 – The Accidental X-ray
Fact: Röntgen's curiosity peaked when a screen glowed unexpectedly in his lab. Unintended exposure led to the discovery of X-rays—and a lifetime supply of airport pat-downs.

1826 – Strike It Lucky
Fact: British chemist John Walker accidentally ignited a chemical-coated stick on his hearth. He'd invented the first match—but never bothered to patent it. Spark of genius, but no royalties.

1849 – Safety Pin for Survival
Fact: Walter Hunt invented the safety pin in just three hours—to pay off a

$15 debt. He sold the patent for $400, while someone else got rich on pins and needles.

1905 – Popsicles by Porch
Fact: Eleven-year-old Frank Epperson left soda mix and a stir stick outside on a freezing night. In the morning—voilà! The first popsicle, invented by a kid and winter weather.

1941 – Nature's Velcro
Fact: After a walk, engineer George de Mestral noticed burrs clinging to his clothes and dog. Under a microscope, those tiny hooks inspired Velcro—thanks, nature!

1853 – Potato Chips: A Salty Revenge
Fact: Chef George Crum sliced potatoes ultra-thin and over-salted them to annoy a complaining customer. The customer loved them. Irony never tasted so crispy.

1942 – Birth Control by Yam
Fact: While studying wild Mexican yams for hormone treatment, Lydia DeWitt accidentally discovered a compound that paved the way for the birth control pill. Talk about plant power.

200 BCE – Fireworks by Bamboo Blast
Fact: Ancient Chinese tossed bamboo into fires and watched it explode from trapped air. Add a few chemicals later, and boom—fireworks were born.

1839 – Vulcanized Rubber by Stove Spill
Fact: Charles Goodyear accidentally dropped rubber and sulfur onto a hot stove. Instead of a gooey mess, he got durable rubber—perfect for tires and a million other things.

1894 – Corn Flakes for Clean Thoughts
Fact: Dr. John Harvey Kellogg invented corn flakes as a bland food to curb, let's say, *unwholesome urges.* They flaked accidentally—and then became breakfast royalty.

1879 – Sticky Innovation: Sandpaper

Fact: Isaac Fischer Jr. spilled sand on sticky paper and noticed it had serious grit. Rather than clean it up, he turned it into sandpaper—woodworkers everywhere thank him.

1905 – Einstein's Patent Office Breakthrough

Fact: At 26, while working in a Swiss patent office, Albert Einstein published his theory of special relativity. The guy literally changed physics on his lunch break.

1870s – The Frisbee Takes Flight

Fact: Yale students began tossing pie tins from Frisbie Baking Company just for fun. That casual toss evolved into the beloved Frisbee—proof that dessert can inspire flight.

🚽 Guess the Idiot

#1 This emperor thought eating pearls dissolved in vinegar was the ultimate flex in luxury dining.

- ☐ A) Nero
- ☐ B) Caligula
- ☐ C) Julius Caesar
- ☐ D) Augustus

#2 This leader banned dancing after dark because he believed it caused earthquakes.

- ☐ A) Chairman Mao
- ☐ B) Kim Jong-il
- ☐ C) Oliver Cromwell
- ☐ D) Napolcon

#3 This king once knighted a penguin at a zoo in a formal military ceremony.

- ☐ A) King Charles III
- ☐ B) King Harald V
- ☐ C) King Olaf V
- ☐ D) King George VI

#4 This ruler built a huge navy... for a kingdom with no coastline.

- ☐ A) King Ludwig II
- ☐ B) Ivan the Terrible

☐ C) Haile Selassie   ☐ D) Frederick William I

#5 This powerful emperor declared war on Neptune, god of the sea, and ordered soldiers to stab the waves.

☐ A) Nero   ☐ C) Napoleon

☐ B) Xerxes I   ☐ D) Caligula

Answers:

1-B, 2-C, 3-B, 4-A, 5-D

Outro

Thank you so much for spending your time with us — and with some of the most bizarre, hilarious, and downright unbelievable moments in history. We don't take it lightly that you chose *this* book to accompany your quiet moments, your curious mind, or maybe just your bathroom breaks. Wherever and however you've been reading, we truly hope it brought you joy.

This book was written with a lot of love, laughter, and fascination for all the strange corners of our past. Our goal was simple: to entertain, surprise, and maybe even spark a "Did you know\...?" conversation that makes someone else laugh as hard as you did. If we managed to make you smile, snort, or shake your head in disbelief — then we did our job right.

If you enjoyed the book, we'd be incredibly grateful if you shared that love. Whether that means leaving a quick review, telling a friend, or gifting it to someone who could use a good laugh, your support helps more than you know. This kind of book spreads best by word of mouth — or maybe word of bathroom.

So, as we close the final page, please know how thankful we are that you came along for the ride. It's been a pleasure writing this for readers like you — the curious, the quirky, and the ones who know that sometimes the best stories... are the strangest ones.

Here's to good laughs, weird history, and the joy of reading — one flush at a time.

Printed in Dunstable, United Kingdom